Allan Armitage
on
Perennials

BURPEE EXPERT
GARDENER SERIES

Allan Armitage

on

Perennials

PRENTICE HALL GARDENING

New York London Toronto Sydney Tokyo Singapore

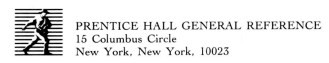

PRENTICE HALL GENERAL REFERENCE
15 Columbus Circle
New York, New York, 10023

Text and photographs copyright © 1993 by Allan Armitage

All photographs by Allan Armitage except photograph on page 109 by Michael Dirr.

PRENTICE HALL and colophon are registered trademarks
of Simon & Schuster, Inc.

BURPEE is a registered trademark of W. Altee Burpee & Company

Library of Congress Cataloging-in-Publication Data

Armitage, A. M. (Allan M.)
    Allan Armitage on perennials / Allan Armitage.
        p.   cm.—(Burpee expert gardener)
    Includes index.
    ISBN 0-671-84722-8
    1. Perennials.   2. Perennials—United States.—I. Title.
    II. Series.
    SB434.A75   1993
    635.9′32—dc20   92-16353
                                                                CIP

Designed by Barbara Cohen Aronica
Manufactured in the United States of America

10 9 8 7 6 5 4 3 2 1

First Edition

Horticultural editor: Suzanne Frutig Bales

Cover: Gardeners may choose the columbine for its color, form or versatility, but the classic elegance of the flower is never in dispute.

Preceding pages: *Rudbeckia triloba* scampering over the author's garden in August.

To my wife, Susan, and my children, Laura, Heather and Jonathan. The joy of gardening pales when compared to the joy of family.

CONTENTS

Lavender and pink make a marvelous combination when Allium stipitatum *(back) and* Persicaria bistorta *(front) are interplanted.*

A FEW THOUGHTS ABOUT GARDENS AND GARDENING

Gardening is different things to different people. To some, gardening is growing a few tomatoes or peppers. Others may prefer to cultivate apples, rhubarb, or okra. I myself am rather useless as a food connoisseur (and much worse as a harvester and preserver), and so most of my garden consists of ornamental plants. The need for a garden is by no means universal, in spite of what gardeners like to believe. Many of my friends and acquaintances view the outside of the house as the "yard," a word that should be reserved for a unit of measurement or in association with prisons. At least the prisoner looks forward to being out in his yard. That cannot be said of many yarders, who see grass only as a job to be done, and plants as necessary evils to hide the foundation of the house. However, one man's yard is another man's garden, and as I walk around my few square yards of heaven, I revel in the sounds of birds, the feeling of serenity, the joy of creativity, and the sight of beauty. Yancy Yardman is as far from my thoughts as I, no doubt, am from his.

When I address garden groups, I see many elderly people in the audience. On garden tours I have led, participants over 60 years of age are not at all uncommon. Seldom have I met an old gardener, though. Elderly and old have nothing to do with each other; elderly is a chronological age, old is an emotion. How many people say, "I feel elderly these days"? Gardening is one of the few endeavors where hope springs eternal. Next year's garden is always going to be better than this year's. Regardless of the time of year, there is always something to anticipate. If the season is winter, the crocus cannot be far behind; in early spring, the wildflowers are just around the corner; approaching summer, the summer-flowering shrubs and daisies are about to burst; and in the fall, ornamental grasses, asters, and fall colors keep us looking forward. When people have something to look forward to, they seldom look back. Gardening keeps us young. Even though our bodies may be raising the white flag of surrender, our minds are still digging in for the battle.

Perennials are but part of the garden. I think they fill an important niche. They constantly change over their season, and this metamorphosis is one of the great joys of gardening. That piece of bare ground in the winter eventually yields leaves, buds, flowers, fruit, and seeds over the course of the season, and in many cases, over the course of a month or two. Perennials can be tucked in little crannies here and there, and they can just as easily dominate the garden. No color is immune from perennials, and wonderful color combinations are possible. I enjoy aspects of garden design, but I am the first to admit that my garden is more of a plantsman's dream and quickly becoming a designer's nightmare. I know in my heart that I should determine the needs for a particular garden spot to complement colors, textures, and heights of other nearby plants. Why is it, then, that I find myself cruising the garden, trowel in one hand and potted plant in the other, searching for any barren ground into which I can plant? I simply can't help myself—I must be a plantomaniac. So many

An old garden bench beckons us into the solitude of a summer garden, a place where time seems to stand still.

Below: *Columbines and foxgloves vie for attention in the afternoon shade in a spring border.*

beautiful perennials are available, and I'd like to try them all. Few designers use my garden as a positive example of their art.

I have gardened in Montreal, Canada, East Lansing, Michigan, and Athens, Georgia, and I can say without hesitation that gardeners always feel their climate is the worst. The same problems with insects, disease, rain, wind, and hail assail all gardens, and if gardeners in Montreal talked with those in Athens, they would find they have a great deal more in common than they believed. But differences do occur. In the South, plants are taller than in the North and plant selection becomes more important. In the South, the season is longer and, while more plants can be used, the gardener should be that much more knowl-

edgeable. Delphiniums and lupines, so wonderful in the northern garden, can be used in the South if planted in the fall for spring flowering and removed with the onset of summer's heat. The most important difference is the length of the hot season. Although Boston and Chicago occasionally swelter in summer heat, Atlanta and Birmingham seem to be in the cooker forever. Plants poorly adapted to such conditions seldom die; they simply languish and eventually end up on the compost heap. Because of hotter summers, planting in the fall is much more important in the South than in the North. The sizzle of a southern summer is made up for by long, pleasant falls, mild winters, and incredible springs. In winter, I used to look out my window in Michigan at

snow blankets; now I find myself wandering through my Georgia garden in January. Although few things are "happening" at that time, the grass is green, the hellebores are budding and the leaves of the arum lilies are fresh. If I could garden in Connecticut in June, July, and August and return to Athens the rest of the year, perhaps I would finally be content. Regardless of where one gardens, there are always memories of beauties past and joy just around the corner. Admire the gardens of others but revel in your own.

Hardiness ratings are provided for all plants discussed in this book. Recently (1990), the United States was divided into 11 zones, based on average minimum temperatures. (See page 176.) This new map supersedes the older 10-zone map used in previous publications. But while making zones more precise, the change in hardiness zones has further confused gardeners. Hardiness ratings should be viewed as guidelines only and not as gospel. Plants can't read, and many a gardener has been successful with plants that should not have survived, let alone flourish, according to the map. Significant differences occur within a single zone, and gardens on the West Coast are quite different in climate from those in the East, although technically they may be in the same zone. Use the hardiness map as one more tool for a successful garden, not as the instruction booklet.

Not long ago, a student approached me for information about my class on herbaceous perennials. She was very interested in environmental concerns and wanted to know if I would be teaching about native plants. I replied that I covered many native plants in my class, but only those I considered worthy of a place in the garden or which showed potential as a commercially available species. She was disappointed, and asked if I didn't believe all native plants to be worthy. As simplistic as that question was, it was surely worth an answer. There need be no argument on the role of native plants in today's world. The value of any living thing is intrinsic; one can place the same value on a toad as on a dandelion. However, the garden value of any plant is in its ability to be effective in that setting. A native plant should not be added to a garden simply because it is native, nor should plant lovers have to trek through pastures, squat by roadsides, or trundle up mountains to enjoy our native flora. I have no quarrel with swamp milkweed as a native plant, but I don't want it in my garden. Native plant purists take exception to the fact that plant breeders have made selections to improve some of the native species. The idea of man interfering in nature's domain is somehow sinister to them, yet these same people marvel at the variation and heterogeneity of plants within a single population on a "nature walk." The only difference between *Echinacea* 'White Swan' and the "pure" species is that 'White Swan' arose as a natural variant in a nursery rather than in a field. The result of that fortunate occurrence is that a white variant of our native species is now enjoyed by many more than those who would have found that field. Similar stories of our native asters, phlox, celandine poppy, iris, lilies, gayfeather, heliopsis, sunflowers, and geraniums can be told. One doesn't have to construct a native garden to enjoy native plants. Many are compatible with hostas from Japan, primroses from the Alps, sages from Tibet, and columbines from Europe. We can't expect people to appreciate and respect native plants if they have to hike to see them or build a garden specifically for them. So many are useful for landscapes and gardens, patios and porches—to make them too special deprives many people of the joy of feeling, smelling, and watching them grow. That nurseries are growing more native plants, species, and selections, provides more reason than ever for incorporating natives in our gardens.

Large masses of Achillea *'The Beacon' cannot help but catch the eye of passersby.*

ABOUT THIS BOOK

The purpose of this book is simply to introduce some of my favorite garden perennials to as many people as possible. Many other wonderful species of perennials available were not included, but I believe the palette of plants chosen includes something for everyone. I have not tried to restrain my passion for many of these plants, and humbly pass that passion on to you. The love of plants and gardening cannot be distilled to sun/shade, easy/difficult, or tall/short components only. While such relevant information is provided for all the plants in the text, this is not meant to be an instruction manual. I have not been able (not that I tried terribly hard) to keep my personal experiences and biases from a few of the plant portraits. My experiences may not mirror yours and some of my dismal failures may have been your greatest triumphs. Enjoy your own triumphs, fleeting though they may be, and don't be unduly concerned with the failures. Two things in life should never be taken seriously: your garden and yourself. Both do much better if we enjoy them more and worry about them less. I hope this book makes your gardening easier, more enjoyable, and provides inspiration for the future.

Each plant portrait provides a reasonable phonetic guide to pronunciation of the botanic name (not necessarily the only correct pronunciation), common name, and approximate hardiness zone limitations. Because taxonomists have disagreed, some plants have more than one botanical name. The colors indicated in the plant portraits really refer to that of the species. Cultivars may exhibit different colors. Tolerance to full sun, partial, or deep shade are also provided. The average hours of sun needed per day is indicated by symbols. The first symbol is what the plant prefers, but the plant is adaptable to all conditions listed.

○ *Sun* — Six hours or more of strong, direct sunlight.

◐ *Partial shade* — Three to six hours of direct sunlight; preferably afternoon shade.

● *Shade* — Two hours or less of direct sunlight.

The text that follows includes information on description, culture, and propagation. The world of gardening is the world of cultivars (or varieties). Many cultivars are a significant improvement on the species and should be grown whenever possible. If cultivars have been selected, some of my favorites are listed with short descriptions of flower color, height, or other ways in which they differ from the species. In some cases, many more cultivars are available than are described. Occasionally I have also snuck in a closely related species because of its useful garden attributes. Finally, an asterisk (°) identifies those plants that are native.

ON THE PROPAGATION OF PERENNIALS

Various means of increasing plants can be used successfully by the gardener and can be accomplished without high-tech tools or elaborate equipment. The four main methods of propagation are by seed, division, stem cuttings, and root cuttings.

The towering spikes of Digitalis purpurea *make a wonderful backdrop for colorful Darwin tulips.*

Seed

Seeds are used for propagation of those true species or cultivars that come relatively true from seed (for example, hybrid columbines, Russell lupines and Pacific hybrid delphiniums). However, many desirable garden cultivars must be asexually propagated. Seeds from many perennials may be germinated easily without elaborate facilities. Four aspects of seed germination must be understood to ensure success.

Fresh Seed

The primary means of survival for many perennials is through overwintering crowns of rootstocks. Seeds formed in summer and fall must germinate rapidly. If germination is slow, seed-lings will be too tender to overwinter. Therefore, seeds will often go dormant if germination conditions are poor. Unfortunately, storing seeds in small foil or paper bags, favorite containers of seed companies, is not a condition to which they are accustomed. Often, purchased seed has already gone dormant and, regardless of how nice the germinating conditions are, will not germinate. Seed dormancy is often a problem with species of certain families and for those that flower later in the summer and fall.

Collecting fresh seeds of problem plants is not always possible. If collected, they must be cleaned from the flower chaff. In general, most seeds germinate more rapidly immediately after ripening and cleaning. However, the following seeds particularly benefit if sown fresh:

Anemone	*Eryngium*
Aster	*Linum*
Cimicifuga	*Pulsatilla*
Delphinium	*Viola*

Conditions to Break Dormancy

Many species do not require any specific pregermination conditions, but some seeds germinate more rapidly and more uniformly with pretreatments.

Stratification. This is a moist, cold treatment that essentially duplicates winter conditions for seeds. Seeds should be stored in moist sand or sown in a moist seed mix and placed in a refrigerator at 35 to 40 degrees Fahrenheit. Generally, a period of four to six weeks is necessary for stratification. Stratification may occur naturally outdoors under snow, in an unheated greenhouse, or in a cold frame. In most cases, stratification can begin immediately after seed has been purchased, but if seed is collected, allow it to ripen at room temperature for two to three weeks. Seeds that benefit from stratification are:

Aconitum	Gentiana
Actaea	Geranium pratense
Alchemilla	Helleborus
Allium	Kirengeshoma
Anemone	Lewisia
Aquilegia	Lilium
Aruncus	Phlox paniculata
Astrantia	Polygonatum
Baptisia	Primula
Bergenia	Pulsatilla
Campanula (some species)	Ranunculus
Cardiocrinum	Rudbeckia laciniata
Chelone	Sanguinaria
Cimicifuga	Saxifraga
Clematis recta	Silene
Dicentra	Tiarella
Dictamnus	Trollius
Eryngium	Veratrum
Erythronium	

Not all species of the above genera benefit from stratification, but it isn't detrimental to them either.

Scarification. This involves making a small cut or abrasion in seeds with hard seed coats in order to help them absorb water more effectively. This can be done with a sharp knife, a nail file, or sandpaper. Soaking in hot water (170 to 210 degrees Fahrenheit) is also effective in softening the seed coat; allow seeds to remain in the soaking water as it cools. Seeds that benefit from scarification are:

Amsonia	Iris
Baptisia	Lathyrus
Canna	Lupinus
Genista	Thermopsis
Hibiscus	

Germination Environment Once Dormancy Is Satisfied

For most seeds, rapid and uniform germination occurs under warm, humid conditions. Constant temperatures of 65 to 75 degrees Fahrenheit enhances germination. Covering the seed tray with a pane of glass or a plastic bag can help keep the temperature and humidity constant; use a fine-mist sprayer to ensure a moist environment for germination. Germination can be done indoors, in a home greenhouse, or in a south-facing cold frame. Humidity is more important than warm temperatures for seed survival; if trays dry out, the seeds will die. If temperatures are too cold, germination is delayed and nonuniform.

These perennials should be sown at cooler temperatures (55 to 65 degrees Fahrenheit):

Arabis	Erigeron
Astilbe	Gypsophila
Aubrieta	Limonium
Aurinia	Lychnis
Campanula	Oenothera
Centaurea	Papaver
Dianthus	Penstemon
Digitalis	Viola

The presence or absence of light is not important for most seeds. Very small seeds should be planted on the surface and barely covered with fine sand or vermiculite (available from hardware stores and garden centers). Larger seeds, those easily handled, may be planted two to three times deeper than their diameter. Some seeds benefit from germination in the dark; they include:

Althaea	*Iris*
Cyclamen	*Lilium*
Hosta	*Pardancanda*

Growing On

Conditions optimal for germination are detrimental to growth once seedlings have emerged. After the first true leaf is visible, the seedlings should be removed from the warm, high-humidity conditions and placed in cooler, brighter conditions. This is necessary to "harden off" the seedlings and is essential for strong growth. One of the most serious problems when gardeners sow their own seed is lack of sufficient light to grow on the seedlings. A cold frame is most useful for seedling development (and much less expensive than a greenhouse).

Fertilize seedlings with a dilute solution (at half the recommended strength) of potassium nitrate (available from garden centers) or a complete fertilizer. Transplant to a bigger pot as soon as the seedlings can be handled. Always handle seedlings by the leaves, not the stem. Once two or three true leaves have formed, fertilization rates can be raised. Plant in the garden when the roots fill the final container, and enjoy the fruits of your labor.

Division

This is the simplest but often the most inefficient method of propagation. Plantlets, with some roots attached, are separated from the "mother" plant. In some cases (*Aster, Boltonia*), literally hundreds of plantlets may be obtained, but with others (*Hemerocallis, Iris*), the mother plant yields only

Some plants live up to their names, as shown here by the snowy effect of a planting of Boltonia asteroides *'Snowbank'.*

one or two divisions. Division is best accomplished in the spring or early fall, although if temperatures are not too hot and water can be provided, division can be done almost anytime during the growing season. Once plantlets have been divided from the mother plant, plant in the garden immediately. The size of the division depends on location, weather, soil, and time of planting.

Cuttings

This means of propagation is often used by the gardener and is invaluable to increase or maintain cultivars that do not divide easily.

Stem cuttings. Taking a cut from the tip of the stem, called the terminal, is a common method of propagation for perennial species. The type of shoot from which the cutting is removed can make a difference in its ability to root. Generally, cuttings taken from the first flush of growth in the spring (basal cuttings) root more easily than tip cuttings taken in midsummer. They may be treated with a rooting hormone containing IBA or NAA (available from garden centers), although such treatments are not necessary for many species. Place cuttings in pots in a well-aerated potting mix, water well, and cover with clear plastic. Place in a sunny window or under fluorescent lights until rooted.

Root cuttings. One can call oneself a big-time gardener when root cuttings are used for propagation. Useful for a few species, root cuttings are the main means of propagation of plants that do not lend themselves to other routine methods. In this method, roots of mother plants are dug and washed in late fall. For gardeners with cold frames or hobby greenhouses, plants may be potted up in the fall and stored until the propagation can be done. (The major exception is *Papaver orientale*, which is propagated in summer while dormant.)

The size of the roots taken depends on the species. *Eryngium* and *Papaver* produce thick fleshy roots, while *Phlox paniculata* produces thin roots. Generally, 1- to 2-inch-long cuttings are sufficient. Fleshy roots should be placed upright. The end of the cutting nearest the crown should be on top, and the tops should be lightly covered. They may be planted directly into 2- to 3-inch-deep pots and rooted in a cold frame or cool greenhouse. With thick roots, such as those of *Anchusa* and *Polygonum*, root pieces may be placed on their side.

Key to the Propagation of Perennials

This basic list of genera provides appropriate propagation methods. With many species, more than one method can be successful. The use of seed is not recommended for hybrids or most named cultivars.

Plant list: C = stem cutting; D = division; R = root cutting; S = seed

Acanthus	DRS
Achillea	DSC
Aconitum	DS
Acorus	D
Aegopodium	D
Agastache	D
Ajuga	D
Alchemilla	DS
Alstroemeria	D
Amsonia	DS
Anaphalis	D
Anchusa	DR
Anemone	DRS
Anemonella	DS
Antennaria	D
Anthemis	DC
Aquilegia	S
Arabis	RDC
Arisaema	DS

Armeria	DSC		Digitalis	DS
Artemisia	CD		Doronicum	DS
Arum	D		Echinacea	RDS
Aruncus	DS		Echinops	SRD
Asarum	DS		Epilobium	DS
Asclepias	SR		Epimedium	D
Asperula	DSC		Erigeron	DCS
Aster	CDS		Eryngium	RD
Asteromea (Kalimeris)	CD		Eupatorium	D
Astilbe	D		Euphorbia	D
Astrantia	DS		Filipendula	D
Aurinia	DC		Gaillardia	RDS
Baptisia	SD		Gaura	S
Belamcanda	DS		Gentiana	DS
Bergenia	SDR		Geranium	DCRS
Boltonia	D		Geum	DS
Borago	D		Gillenia	DS
Boykinia	D		Gypsophila	C
Brunnera	DRS		Helenium	D
Campanula	DSC		Helianthus	D
Canna	DS		Heliopsis	DCS
Caryopteris	CS		Helleborus	S
Catananche	RSD		Hemerocallis	DS
Centaurea	DRS		Hesperis	SD
Cerastium	DSC		Heuchera	D
Ceratostigma	CSD		Hibiscus	D
Chelone	D		Hosta	D
Chrysanthemum	DSC		Houttuynia	D
Chrysogonum	D		Hypericum	D
Cimicifuga	DS		Iberis	C
Clematis	CDS		Incarvillea	RS
Codonopsis	DS		Inula	D
Convallaria	D		Iris	DS
Coreopsis	D		Kirengeshoma	DS
Corydalis	DS		Kniphofia	DS
Crambe	RD		Lamiastrum	DC
Crocosmia	D		Lamium	DC
Cyclamen	D		Lavandula	DC
Cynoglossum	DS		Lewisia	S
Delphinium	SCD		Liatris	D
Dianthus	DCS		Ligularia	D
Dicentra	RD		Linum	SC
Dictamnus	RS		Liriope	D

Lobelia	DS		Sisyrinchium	DS
Lupinus	SC		Solidago	DC
Lychnis	DS		Solidaster	DC
Lysimachia	DSC		Stachys	DS
Lythrum	DSC		Stokesia	RDS
Macleaya	DR		Stylophorum	S
Mertensia	RDS		Symphytum	RDS
Monarda	DC		Teucrium	CDS
Myosotis	DC		Thalictrum	DS
Nepeta	DC		Thermopsis	DS
Oenothera	RSD		Thymus	D
Pachysandra	DC		Tiarella	DS
Paeonia	D		Tradescantia	D
Papaver	RSD		Tricyrtis	DS
Penstemon	DC		Trillium	DS
Perovskia	CDS		Trollius	RD
Phlox	RDCS		Uvularia	D
Physostegia	DSC		Veratrum	D
Platycodon	CS		Verbascum	DRS
Polemonium	DS		Verbena	DS
Polygonatum	D		Vernonia	D
Polygonum	RD		Veronica	DCS
Potentilla	DS		Veronicastrum	D
Primula	DSR		Vinca	DC
Pulmonaria	DRS		Viola	DSC
Pulsatilla	RS		Waldsteinia	D
Rodgersia	DS		Zephyranthes	D
Rudbeckia	DS			
Salvia	DCS			
Sanguisorba	DS			
Santolina	CS			
Saponaria	RDC			
Scabiosa	DS			
Schizostylis	D			
Sedum	DC			
Sempervivum	DS			
Silene	D			

For gardeners who want additional in-depth information about many, many more genera and species of perennials, you may refer to *Herbaceous Perennial Plants*, my 640-page reference for gardeners who can't get enough. Available through Timber Press, 9999 S.W. Wilshire, Portland, OR 97225, it should help to fill in a few more gaps in perennial plant knowledge.

The flowers of Papaver somniferum, *the opium poppy, can provide some of the most spectacular color in the garden (page 124).*

PLANT PORTRAITS

Beautiful but painful to the touch, Acanthus spinosus *var.* spinosissimus *is best admired from a distance.*

ACANTHUS (A-KANTH-us)
Bear's Breeches

The flowers and foliage of plants in this genus are equally attractive, although some species have spiny leaf margins and can be lethal if inadvertently touched. For me, the evergreen foliage is more handsome than the purplish-green spiny flower stalks; however, half the fun of growing any plant is to discover the interest of the flowers. The roots of bear's breeches are long-lived, and if you decide that you don't like the plants anymore, you may be in trouble. They are notoriously difficult to remove because every remaining piece of root results in little breechlets. *Acanthus* grows particularly well on the West Coast, but is also popular in southern areas of the country. "The books" say that it is winter hardy to Zone 7 or 8 but *Acanthus* is a perfect example of a plant that can't read. I couldn't believe my eyes when I saw the marvelous well-established clumps of bear's breeches at Gardenview Horticultural Park in Strongsville, Ohio. (This marvelous garden, about 30 minutes outside Cleveland, is the passion of Henry Ross, an opinionated plantsman whose love of plants shows as soon as you enter the gates.) Flourishing in Zone 5, *Acanthus* is living proof that plants should be tried even in places where "experts" disagree. All *Acanthus* species require full sun to be at their best, although plants in my Georgia garden are in partial shade and appear to be reasonably happy. Plants are commonly propagated from root cuttings, although division and seed are also used. Take 2- to 3-inch-long pieces of strong roots and insert them vertically in a well-drained medium. Division is best accomplished in early spring. Sowing seed in January in a warm (70° to 75° Fahrenheit.), moist area will provide seedlings for spring transplants.

BALCANICUS (BAL-can-I-CUS)
Balcan Bear's Breeches
Color: Purple and white
Zones: 6 to 9

This is an outstanding newcomer to American gardening. The rich green foliage is deeply cut like that of *A. spinosus* but is not spiny. Plants are wonderfully tolerant of summer heat and humidity and the spring-to-early-summer flowers are reliable. Plants have performed well in my garden for three years. Their only drawback is a tendency to wilt in the afternoon sun. Provide afternoon shade if possible, particularly in the South, and do not allow the soil to dry out completely.

MOLLIS (MOL-LIS)
Common Bear's Breeches
Color: Purple and white
Zones: 6 to 9

Folklore suggests that it is the foliage of this species that was immortalized as the sculpted leaves on Greek Corinthian columns in the fifth century B.C. Not being a student of Greek architecture, I cannot dispute that claim, but still I have to use my imagination a great deal when I see those columns of Corinth. Plants have wavy, lustrous green leaves without spines; the flower stem, which carries numerous white and purple flowers in the spring, does bear spiny bracts. The flower stem rises 3 to 4 feet above the low-growing foliage and if three or more plants are placed together, they can be very attractive. The foliage is winter hardy to Zone 6, but flowers seldom appear in my garden. Plants are less tolerant of hot or cold weather and less attractive than their cousins, *A. spinosus* and *A. balcanicus*.

SPINOSUS (SPINE-O-SUS)
Spiny Bear's Breeches
Color: Purple
Zones: 7 to 10

The margins of the leaves in this species have small spines, much less lethal than they appear. Plants are tolerant of winter freezes. The foliage remains healthier through the season and plants flower more consistently than *A. mollis*; the foliage is more deeply divided than that of *mollis*, but the flowers are essentially the same. This is an excellent plant, not only for the West Coast, but also for the South and East.

The deep yellow flowers of Achillea filipendulina *'Gold Plate' make a wonderful foreground for the red flowers of* Lychnis chalcedonica *(Maltese-cross) and sulphur flowers of* Thalictrum speciosissimum.

ACHILLEA (A-KIL-LEE-A)
Yarrow

Many species and colors of yarrow are available to today's gardeners due to selection and breeding efforts throughout the world. The foliage of many species is deeply cut and has a spicy fragrance. These plants range in height from 4 inches to 4 feet and may be enjoyed as garden plants, fresh-cut flowers, or dried everlastings. If flowers are to be cut, be sure to wait until they are fully open or vase life will be poor. All species require full sun and well-drained soils, but if fertilized too heavily, plants may become lanky and leggy. Some yarrows are best at the front of the garden, whereas some of the taller ones are most effective standing guard in the middle or back of the border. Plants of all species are easily grown from seed, but division of the low-growing species is almost foolproof and may be done anytime. A small division with a piece of root is all that is required to propagate most of the species. Terminal cuttings, particularly of the upright species, may also be used.

'CORONATION GOLD'
Coronation Gold Yarrow
Color: Yellow
Zones: 3 to 9
◯

This hybrid (*A. clypeolata* × *A. filipendulina*) is one of the finest upright, yellow-flowering yarrows available today. Due to its hybrid nature, plants are vigorous, well branched and compact. They do not require staking and are hardy from southern Canada to northern Florida. Plants grow to 3 feet in height and are excellent for landscapers wanting a low-maintenance, reliable plant for late spring and summer flowering. As a cut flower, it is used fresh and may also be dried (in a warm, well-ventilated area) to yield colorful everlasting bouquets.

FILIPENDULINA
(FI-LI-PEN-DEW-LYE-NA)
Fernleaf Yarrow
Color: Yellow
Zones: 3 to 9
◯

Plants are similar to the above hybrid, but they are taller (3 to 5 feet) and bear fewer but larger, more striking flowers. The height makes this an excellent yellow-flowering yarrow for the middle or back of the garden. The handsome, light green foliage is deeply cut and provides an airy foil to the coarser leaves of many other species. Plants are at their best in early summer and look particularly attractive in concert with the blue balloon flower, *Platycodon grandiflorus*. Plants are all easily propagated from seed and division. One of the easiest and prettiest flowers for the summer garden.

Cultivars

'Gold Plate' has deep yellow flowers on stems 5 feet tall.

'Parker's Variety' bears golden yellow flowers on stems 3 to 4 feet tall. Both cultivars produce stronger stems and slightly larger flowers than the species. Both can be seed-propagated.

MILLEFOLIUM
(MIL-LEE-FO-LEE-UM)
Common Yarrow
Colors: Various
Zones: 3 to 9
◯

This species of yarrow spreads by underground stems so rapidly that it quickly becomes "common," thus its common name. Plants bear finely dissected dark green foliage, above which arise many 8- to 12-inch-long flower stalks. Selection and breeding have resulted in a rainbow of flower colors, ranging from white to red and all shades between. In cooler climates, plants can look outstanding most of the season; in areas of hot summers, however, plants tend to become leggy and the foliage deteriorates somewhat. The flowers are brighter and the stems thicker in areas where night temperatures consistently fall below 70 degrees Fahrenheit. Common yarrow is an excellent choice for the front of the garden. Fertilize sparingly. Plants may be propagated easily by division any time of the year but spring is the best season. Many cultivars can also be propagated from seed. The colors will not be as uniform as with divisions, but many more plants can be raised.

Cultivars

'Cerise Queen' is 15 to 20 inches tall and bears cerise red flowers in large drifts.

'Fire Beauty' and 'Fire King' bear dark red flowers. There appears to be little difference between them.

'Paprika' is an excellent red-and-white bicolor. This relatively new cultivar, which may be a hybrid, has an exceptionally bright future.

'Red Beauty' (rose-red) and 'Rose Beauty' ('Rosea') are popular, rapidly spreading cultivars.

'Summer Pastels' comes in an assortment of pastel colors and shades. An All-American award winner.

'Wesersandstein' is a handsome cultivar with rose-pink flowers.

Other Hybrids

Numerous hybrids have *A. millefolium* as a parent. The Galaxy series (*A. millefolium* × *A. taygetea*) is one of the finest group of hybrid yarrows for the garden. Cultivars include 'Appleblossom' (pink), 'Great Expectations' ('Hope', sandstone yellow), 'Salmon Beauty' (salmon-pink) and 'The Beacon' ('Fanal', red). All have been extensively tested and although flowers tend to fade in the heat of the summer, plants are vigorous, easily grown, and bear larger flowers than the species. All may be propagated any time from division.

As a garden plant, Acidanthera bicolor *provides beauty and fragrance; as a cut flower it has few equals.*

ACIDANTHERA
(A-SID-AN-THE-RA)
Abyssinian Gladiolus

Only one species of *Acidanthera* is commonly available. These bulbs are underused and relatively unknown by American gardeners. The bulbs are so inexpensive that all gardeners can afford to try a few.

BICOLOR (BI-KO-LOR)
Abyssinian Gladiolus
Color: White with purple throat
Zones: 7 to 10

The flared white flowers have deep purple throats and are borne up the 3-foot-tall stem in a manner similar to that of other gladioli. Not only are they handsome, but they possess a light, haunting fragrance. Stems may be cut to provide excellent flowers that persist five to seven days in water. Bulbs, except those in the Deep South, need to be lifted (like gladioli). Lift after the first frost, remove the foliage, and gently clean the soil from the bulbs. Sort the large bulbs from the smaller bulblets and store in a well-ventilated area at 40 to 50 degrees Fahrenheit. Dipping bulbs in an all-purpose fungicide helps reduce disease during storage. Plant in early spring after the last frost. For lazy gardeners like myself, treat bulbs like annuals—that is, discard the bulbs after the first season and replace the next spring. If bulbs overwinter in the ground (Zone 7 south), they often produce far more foliage than flowers.

Cultivars

'Muralis' bears larger flowers on stronger stems than the species. Plant grows to 3½ feet tall.

The spires of Aconitum carmichaelii 'Arendsii' *stand guard over a quiet border in New England.*

ACONITUM (A-KO-NY-TUM)
Monkshood, Wolfsbane

The common names for the genus are both descriptive and gruesome. The name monkshood is in reference to the shape of the flower, which indeed resembles a cowl or monk's hood. The other common name, wolfsbane, arose from the poisonous properties of the roots and their ability to thin wolf populations. The fact that *Aconitum* is poisonous has sometimes been an impediment to its use in American gardens, but if people don't grovel around trying to eat the roots, or mistake them for sweet potatoes, it is as safe as salvia. After all, how many gardeners raise sweet potatoes and monkshood in the same plot?

The foliage is divided into many sections and is handsome in its own right. Flowers are generally in shades of deep blue, although cream-colored blooms occasionally are produced. They are borne on tall flower spikes in late summer and fall. They are truly magnificent spires of the late-season garden. Flowers are also excellent as cut flowers and persist for many days if placed in a clean vase with floral preservative. Unfortunately, monkshood doesn't grow particularly well south of Zone 6 due to warm summer temperatures, an unfortunate limit to its popularity, and it is sorely missed in the Armitage garden.

CARMICHAELII
(KAR-MY-KEEL-LEE-EYE)
Azure Monkshood
Color: Dark blue
Zones: 3 to 7
○

These sturdy plants seldom need staking (a problem not uncommon with other species) and bear lovely dark blue flowers in late summer and fall. Plant in soils generously amended with organic matter and leave the plants undisturbed for best performance. When combined with Japanese anemones and fall sedums, they are a knockout.

Cultivars

'Arendsii', which may be a hybrid between *A. carmichaelii* and its var. *wilsonii*, bears large helmets of intense blue on 3- to 4-foot-tall stems. Sturdy, self-supporting, and elegant, this plant is outstanding.

'Baker's Variety' has deep blue flowers and is a cultivar of var. *wilsonii*. It can grow to 6 feet in height under ideal conditions.

NAPELLUS (NA-PEL-LUS)
Common Monkshood
Color: Deep blue
Zones: 3 to 7
○

The most common monkshood available, this is outstanding when grown in groups of three or more. Normally 3 to 4 feet tall, the plant produces numerous deep blue flowers along the stout flower stem. This is a common cut flower in floral markets in Europe and the northwestern United States. Place where plants will not be disturbed. The tuberous roots are long-lived and plants persist for 10 years if properly sited in a cool, moist garden location.

Cultivars

'Carneum', listed by some authorities as a cultivar of *A. compactum*, bears pink flowers, an unusual flower color for this genus. The plants do poorly unless grown in consistently cool climates (such as the Northeast and Northwest), with the pink flowers fading in warm weather.

'Newry Blue' bears many noble spires of mid- to deep blue. Plants grow 4 feet tall.

ORIENTALE (ORE-EE-EN-TALL)
Creamy Monkshood
Color: Sulphur yellow
Zones: 3 to 6
○

The sulphur-colored flowers of this species are held on 4- to 6-foot-tall dense, branched racemes above divided leaves. Plants are not as strong or upright as other species, but if placed toward the back of the garden and allowed to sprawl over neighbors, they are magnificent in late summer and fall. The fibrous roots are not as persistent as those of *A. napellus*, but the plants are still relatively long-lived. One quickly acquires a deep appreciation of *Aconitum* after seeing this species in its glory.

The bronze leaves of Ajuga reptans *'Atropurpurea' contrast well with the lavender flowers in this spring garden.*

AJUGA (A-JEW-GAH)
Bugleweed

Of approximately 30 species of bugleweed, only 3 are found to any extent in American gardens. All *Ajuga* species are excellent groundcovers for a partially shaded location. The most common species, *A. reptans* (common bugleweed), is available in numerous flower colors and in a magnificent palette of foliage hues. Propagating anytime by division is the easiest means of increasing plant numbers.

REPTANS (REP-TANZ)
Common Bugleweed
Color: Blue
Zones: 3 to 9

This is one of my favorite groundcovers for areas in full sun to partial shade. The plants remain short (6 to 9 inches tall) and fill in within two to three years. Although often selected for foliage color, flowers are magnificent as plantings become larger. Deep blue oceans of color in spring draw the gardener's attention. The foliage of the more colorful cultivars, even after flowers have disappeared, is also wonderful. However, with this pleasure also comes the nightmare of seeing these plants overrun adjacent areas. This is particularly true when plants are placed at the front of a garden that borders the lawn. (The helpless feeling of watching bugleweed take over the lawn could lead a gardener to drink.) Buglelawn, as this condition has become known, is a common failing of the overenthusiastic bugleite.

Cultivars

Selected for Flower Color

'Alba' has creamy white flowers.

'Catlin's Giant' has long (up to 8 inches) spikes of blue flowers and bronze-green leaves.

'Pink Beauty' bears 4- to 5-inch-long spikes of deep pink flowers and green foliage. This plant is sometimes listed as a cultivar of *A. genevensis* (Geneva bugleweed).

'Pink Spire' has lovely pink flowers atop green foliage.

Selected for Foliage Color

'Bronze Beauty' produces drifts of metallic bronze foliage.

'Burgundy Glow' has foliage in shades of white, pink, rose, and green. The older leaves turn deep bronze in the fall. A popular, although gaudy, cultivar for the landscape.

'Gaiety' has bronze leaves and lilac flowers.

'Jungle Beauty Improved' bears mahogany-purple leaves and blue flowers.

'Silver Beauty' has gray-green leaves edged with white.

The flowers of Alchemilla mollis *not only brighten the garden but make wonderful cut flowers as well.*

ALCHEMILLA (AL-KEM-ILL-A)
Lady's-Mantle

Lady's-mantle has been in European gardens forever but only in the last 10 years has it made a significant impact on American horticulture. The light green, lobed foliage makes a magnificent edging along pathways, and a small grouping of plants at the front of the garden shows off the leaves and yellow-green flowers in the spring. The flowers are made up of sepals only (no petals) and may be brought in the house as a filler for more showy cut flowers on display. Approximately 30 species of lady's-mantle exist, including such useful species as *A. alpina* (alpine lady's-mantle) and *A. erythropoda* (hairy lady's-mantle). However, the most popular and easiest to locate species is *A. mollis* (common lady's-mantle).

ALPINA (AL-PINE-A)
Alpine Lady's-Mantle
Color: Yellow-green
Zones: 4 to 7

Alpine lady's-mantle has silvery margins and undersides to the leaves and is smaller and (in my opinion) more handsome than common lady's-mantle. Plants are more suitable for the rock garden. A wonderful plant, even relatively tolerant of summer heat and humidity.

MOLLIS (MOL-LIS)
Common Lady's-Mantle
Color: Yellow-green
Zones: 4 to 7

Introduced into European cultivation in 1874 from the mountains of Asia Minor, the species has enjoyed immense popularity as an informal groundcover. The large, round, shallowly lobed leaves, evenly covered with hairs, are handsome throughout the season. The conspicuous green-yellow inflorescences flow from the crown of the plant to fall over and rest on the light green foliage. Plants are more robust in cooler areas of the country than in the South. Hot, humid temperatures, in combination with abundant summer rain, result in problems because water droplets tend to get caught in the hairy leaves and leaf rot sets in. Plants south of Zone 6 do not have the vigor of those grown farther north. However, all is relative; if you haven't grown lady's-mantle before, it will look nice wherever you live. It is in its glory in the spring, when the flowers are most apparent, but if moisture is maintained, the foliage is always handsome.

Like large fuzzy tennis balls, the flowers of Allium karataviense *sit atop fleshy green leaves in the spring.*

Brilliant purple globes of Allium aflatunense *'Purple Sensation' look down upon other plants in a small garden in the Midwest.*

ALLIUM (AL-LEE-um)
Ornamental Onion

Gardening, to many people, is growing vegetables. To these folks, tomatoes, cucumbers, and squash are the epitome of gardening. Their rallying cry seems to be "if you can't eat them, why grow them?" I finally became marginally acceptable to my vegetable-gardening friends when I started growing onions, albeit the ornamental kind. The large pool of ornamental onions available to the gardener is staggering and the beauties of many are relatively unknown. Alliums range from early-spring bloomers such as *A. christophii* to the autumn-flowering *A. thunbergii*, and grow from the 2- to 3-inch *A. circinatum* to the 4-foot-tall giant onion *A. giganteum*. They don't smell of onions unless crushed and, in fact, flowers of some species have a pleasant fragrance. Bulbs of all species should be planted in the fall, approximately three times deeper than the diameter of the bulb. When planted in full sun and relatively well-drained soils, bulbs persist for many years. They should be placed in groupings of at least five bulbs for best results. Most tall species make excellent cut flowers, fresh or dry, and if placed in clean water, flourish for many weeks. Propagation is accomplished from bulblets, which may be divided and separated by size immediately after flowering.

CHRISTOPHII (KRIS-TOF-EE-EYE)

Downy Onion, Star of Persia

Color: Lilac

Zones: 4 to 8

○

A terrific low-growing onion, the 10-inch-diameter metallic lilac flower heads dwarf the plant in early spring. Each small star-shaped flower is only about ½ inch wide but the flower head consists of 80 to 100 such flowers. The plants normally stand 1½ to 2 feet tall and the two to four strap-shaped leaves disappear quickly after flowering has finished. For head-turning appeal, this species is hard to beat.

GIGANTEUM (GI-GAN-TEE-UM)

Giant Onion

Color: Purple

Zones: 4 to 8

○

The common name only hints at the size of this beast. The large bulb produces 4- to 6-foot-tall flower stalks above 6 to 9 straplike basal leaves. The foliage starts to decline even before the flowers are fully open. Place the bulbs in the midst of other leafy perennials or small shrubs that will hide the fading foliage and declining stems after flowering. The flower heads consist of hundreds of tightly packed ½-inch-wide flowers that form perfectly rounded 6- to 8-inch-diameter purple balls atop tall gangly stems. Planted in groups of six or more, these plants look like a small colony of my daughter's drawings of stick men. The stems may be cut and are wonderful as fresh or dried flowers, in constant demand by florists and floral arrangers.

KARATAVIENSE (KA-RA-TAH-VEE-EN-SE)

Turkestan Onion

Color: Silver-lilac

Zones: 4 to 8

○

Grown for the foliage almost as much as the flowers, this low-growing (6- to 12-inch) perennial is great fun to have in the garden. The leaves are up to 4 inches wide and mottled purple, particularly on the undersides and near the base. The round silver-lilac flower heads are 8 to 10 inches across and borne on sturdy 6- to 9-inch-tall stems. These plants are particularly handsome planted through a groundcover such as *Verbena peruviana* or, as is the case at Denver Botanical Garden, through a beautiful carpet of *Veronica liwanensis*.

MOLY (MAH-LEE)

Lily Leek, Golden Onion

Color: Yellow

Zones: 3 to 9

○

If golden yellow flowers in early to midspring are desired, *A. moly*'s numerous ½-inch-wide star-shaped flowers on 2-inch-diameter inflorescences can be the answer. The 12- to 15-inch plants bear blue-green flat leaves that do not detract from the beauty of the flower and disappear rapidly after flowering. Plant about a dozen bulbs in the fall and enjoy the golden vista the following spring.

Cultivars

'Jeannine' is taller (12 to 18 inches), more vigorous, and bears brighter yellow flowers than the species. An excellent improvement and highly recommended.

The pale blue flowers of Amsonia tabernaemontana *open over fresh greenery in a partially shaded garden.*

* *AMSONIA* (AM-SOWN-EE-AH)
Blue Starflower

A terribly overlooked genus, *Amsonia* consists of approximately seven species native to North America. While the flowers of most species are light blue and occur in the spring, the foliage provides beauty year 'round. Early flowering, lack of diseases and pests, and fine foliage throughout the season make this genus a winner.

HUBRECTII
(HUE-BRECK-TEE-EYE)
Arkansas Amsonia
Color: Light blue
Zones: 6 to 8

Golden drifts of this plant, providing fall color equal to that of many maples, open one's eyes to the possibility of using herbaceous perennials for fall color. The light blue flowers occur over thin grasslike foliage in the spring. Plants may become too tall if placed in shade; cut back if necessary after the first flush of flowers. Propagate anytime by division or cutting.

TABERNAEMONTANA
(TAY-BER-NAY-MON-TAN-A)
Willow Amsonia
Color: Pale blue
Zones: 3 to 9

Adaptable to a wide range of climates and soils, these plants flourish from Chicago, Illinois, to Athens, Georgia. The pale blue starflowers open early in spring and persist for three to four weeks. The narrow leaves are ornamental from the time they emerge until they turn golden yellow in the fall. The plants grandly lining the stairs in the Waterfall Garden at the Chicago Botanical Garden are particularly impressive in

October, but even my own plants in Georgia provide a lovely fall display. Place in full sun for best results; if too much shade is present, plants become leggy and require cutting back after flowering. (I grow them through a support ring because I have too much shade.) No cutting back is necessary and the foliage remains handsome all season.

Cultivars

Var. *montana* is a dwarf version of the species, standing only 12 to 15 inches tall. It is sometimes listed as *A. montana* but regardless of the listing, it is an exceptional plant, particularly for the South. I have seen beautiful specimens in many gardens and recommend this plant highly.

Anchusa azurea 'Loddon Royalist' dominates the summer border.

ANCHUSA (AN-KOO-SA)
Alkanet

Numerous species of *Anchusa* occur but only one is readily available to the American gardener. All species are hairy throughout and generally bear blue to purple flowers in the spring or early summer. Flowers open like slowly uncurling scorpion tails. Most cultivars are short lived and, although impressive when well grown, seldom persist more than three years.

AZUREA (A-ZEWR-REE-A)
Italian Alkanet
Color: Deep blue
Zones: 3 to 8
○

This tall-growing, coarsely hairy species makes an excellent backdrop to smaller spring-flowering plants. The ½- to ¾-inch-wide spring flowers are a welcome sight amidst the coarse foliage. Plants grow 3 to 5 feet tall and 3 feet wide, but 1- to 2-foot-tall cultivars are also available. In the North, the shades of blue are almost electric in their intensity. Propagate by seed or by root cuttings. Two- to 3-inch-long pieces of healthy root cuttings should be horizontally inserted in moist, well-drained potting soils and maintained at 70 to 75 degrees Fahrenheit.

Cultivars

'Dropmore' bears deep blue flowers on plants 4 feet tall. Plants require a good deal of room in the garden and become rather untidy after flowering.

'Little John' is only 1½ feet tall with dark blue flowers. An excellent dwarf version of the species.

'Loddon Royalist' has gentian blue flowers over 3-foot-tall plants. Some of the finest plants I have seen were in the garden of Sir John Thueron, outside Philadelphia. Standing like sentinels, they guarded the integrity of the perennial border, even in 90-degree heat.

'Opal' is 3 to 4 feet tall and bears azure blue flowers.

ANEMONE (A-NEM-O-NEE)
Windflower

Few groups of plants offer as much diversity as those of *Anemone*. From the early-spring-flowering, tuberous-rooted Grecian windflower to the fall-flowering hybrids, anemones can provide something for everyone in at least one season of the year. Most species have compound foliage and flowers whose showy part consists of sepals only (no petals). All appreciate some

Plants of Anemone vitifolia *'Robustissima' (A.* tomentosa*) flower in late summer and fall and are some of the most fool-proof perennials to grow.*

protection from wind and afternoon sun and do poorly if allowed to dry out. Propagate the tuberous types by lifting the tubers after flowering and dividing with a sharp knife. Other species may be propagated by division or root cuttings.

BLANDA (BLAN-DA)
Grecian Windflower
Colors: Various
Zones: 4 to 8

A useful little species, it is one of the earliest flowers to greet the spring (late winter, in many areas). The 1- to 2-inch-wide flowers consist of many narrow ½-inch-long sepals around a small colored center. If heavily planted, a 6- to 8-inch-tall floral carpet appears in early spring. Plant at least 25 tubers in the fall, 1 to 3 inches apart, for an impressive show; place tubers about 3 inches below the surface in well-drained soil.

Cultivars

'Blue Star' has 2- to 2½-inch-wide dark blue flowers.

'Bridesmaid' bears white flowers.

'Charmer' has 2-inch-wide pale pink ray flowers around a white center.

'Pink Star' consists of pink-purple flowers about 9 inches tall.

'Radar' produces many large mauve flowers with white centers and is one of the most handsome cultivars available.

'White Splendour' is very popular with gardeners looking for a clean white spring flower.

Replant the tubers of Anemone coronaria *'De Caen' every one or two years for best garden performance.*

CORONARIA (KO-RO-NAH-REE-A)
Poppy Anemone
Colors: Various
Zones: 6 to 9

This species provides some of the largest and most handsome flowers in the genus. The colorful flowers have been cultivated as cut flowers in the greenhouse and field for many years and continue to be popular with florists. The finely divided foliage may emerge in the fall after planting, depending on climate, and flowers arise in late winter or early spring. Plant tubers 3 inches deep in the fall (October to November) after soaking overnight in water. Placing them in a shady area has no effect on the number of flowers formed but increases the length of the flower stem, a useful trick if growing anemones for cut flowers. Flowering declines rapidly and plants start to go dormant once temperatures begin to rise in the spring. Although plants may continue to flower for two to three years, flowing declines over time. I treat these inexpensive tubers as annuals and replant most years; however, north of Zone 6 they may be dug and replanted in late winter or early spring.

Cultivars

'De Caen' hybrids, developed in the Caen district of France, bear single, saucer-shaped 2- to 3-inch-wide flowers on 8- to 10-inch-tall stems. They are available in single colors or as a mix.

'Mona Lisa' was developed for cut flowers for the greenhouse industry and produces large colorful flowers on 15-inch stems. Flowers have excellent vase life, superior to 'De Caen', but are more expensive and difficult to locate.

'St. Brigid' has semidouble flowers available in mixed or single colors.

Song Bird series consists of some exceptionally handsome cultivars named after birds. 'Blue Bird' (light blue and white), 'Blue Jay' (dark blue and white), 'Dove' (pink and white) and 'Cardinal' (violet and white) are but a sampling of this wonderful series. Plants are 2 to 3 feet tall and highly recommended by this gardener.

All hybrids may be purchased as seed, but seed collected from garden plants will likely not produce flowers similar to the parent's.

VULGARIS (VUL-GAH-RIS)
Granny's Bonnet
Colors: Blue, white and violet
Zones: 3 to 8

Although often used as a parent for numerous hybrids, this species boasts considerable charm of its own. The 1½- to 2-foot-tall plants display tremendous flower variation, but in general they are blue or violet, with short inward-curving spurs ending in small knobs. Plants are durable and persist well in areas of warm summer temperatures. Plant in partial shade and well-drained soil. Drainage is so critical that plants have been known to grow on rock outcrops. Double and near-triple forms exist—some of the ugliest flowers in the plant kingdom.

Cultivars

'Nivea' is about 3 feet tall and bears single white flowers over gray-green foliage. Gertrude Jekyll, a well-known English gardener, used this variety so much that it came to be known as the Munstead white columbine, in hommage to her garden, Munstead Woods.

Shady, moist conditions are perfect for this early-flowering "Jack-in-the-pulpit," Arisaema sikokianum.

ARISAEMA (A-WRIS-AYE-MA)
Jack-in-the-Pulpit

Generally one doesn't think of jack-in-the-pulpit as a big-time perennial. However, "jacks" make excellent plants for the shaded garden. I love to try different species (approximately 100 are available) because they are unique and never fail to impress.

SIKOKIANUM (SI-COKE-EE-AYE-NUM)

Japanese Jack-in-the-Pulpit

Color: White

Zones: 5 to 8

This is one of my favorite jacks, a magnificent species native to Japan. The flowers consist of a cloaklike structure called a spathe, within which is the narrow flower spike (the spadix, or jack). The 6- to 10-inch spathe is deep purple with narrow green bands. The bands have a purplish line on the outside and are flecked with dark purple within. The white jack within is about 2 inches long. It looks a great deal better than it sounds. Plants emerge and flower at least four weeks earlier than the native jacks in my garden and flowers have almost disappeared by the time flowers of *A. triphyllum* have emerged. The one disadvantage is that flowers may be damaged by late frosts. Hardiness limits have not been well defined, but this plant is likely hardy to Zone 5. If you can find these, try them.

* TRIPHYLLUM (TRY-FILL-UM)

Common Jack-in-the-Pulpit

Colors: Green to maroon

Zones: 3 to 8

This most common species is native to large areas of eastern North America, and is well known for the three-parted leaves and the large green-to-purplish-brown-striped hoodlike spathe. Flowers, made up of the elongated spadix (jack) and surrounding 4- to 6-inch-long spathe (pulpit), emerge in the spring. After the spathe withers, green berries form and turn bright orange in late summer and fall, and finally the entire plant goes dormant. Plants require constantly moist garden soil and moderate shade. In my garden, plants are 3 feet tall and gorgeous. If soils dry out or temperatures are too warm, plants go dormant early and fruit set is poor. All species are tuberous and easily transplanted once dormancy has occurred.

Rose-pink flowers of Armeria maritima *spill over the rock garden at Longwood Gardens in Kennett Square, PA.*

ARMERIA (AR-MEER-ee-a)
Sea Thrift

Of approximately 50 known species, *A. maritima* (common sea thrift) is the most useful for the garden. Sea thrift is so named because the species is undaunted by salt spray; this is one of the few garden plants that tolerates coastal conditions. The 1- to 1½-inch-diameter rounded flower heads, which may be lilac, rose, or white, are made up of many tiny flowers attached to a central flower dome. The foliage grows from the base only (basal), and consists of a tuft of 4- to 8-inch-long narrow leaves, each with a prominent mid-vein. Plants are excellent for the rock garden or edge of the flower garden. Provide full sun in the North, partial shade in the South. Although hardy from Zone 4 to Zone 8, they do not thrive in the heat of the South as well as they thrive in the North.

Cultivars

'Alba' is 4 to 6 inches tall with creamy white flowers.

'Bloodstone' bears deep pink flowers on plants 8 to 10 inches tall.

'Dusseldorf Pride' ('Düsseldorfer Stolz') grows 6 to 8 inches tall and bears large, wine red flower heads.

'Laucheana' produces a highly tufted rosette of leaves and deep rose flowers on 6-inch stems.

'Robusta' is one of the most vigorous cultivars. The plant grows 12 to 18 inches tall and bears 3-inch-wide pink flower heads.

'Ruby Glow' has flowers similar to 'Dusseldorf Pride' and is 8 to 10 inches tall.

'Splendens' has intense red flowers—an excellent cultivar.

'Vindictive' is compact, growing only about 6 inches tall, and bears bright rosy red flowers. (A terrible name for a lovely plant.)

ARTEMISIA (ARE-ti-MEEZ-ee-a)
Wormwood

There are so many useful species (over 200 are known) of *Artemisia* that it is difficult to select a handful of the best. This genus has provided such famous members as *A. dracunculus* (tarragon), *A. tridentata* (tumbling sagebrush), and *A. absinthium* (absinthe). Flowers are inconspicuous or lacking (except in *A. lactiflora*), and plants are much more useful for the aromatic gray-green, much divided foliage. The foliage is a designer's dream, a calming mediator among harsher colors in the perennial garden. Place in full sun, although plants tolerate partial shade, and grow on the lean, dry side. Propagate by terminal cuttings in spring or with heel cuttings (cuttings with small pieces of stem) in late summer and fall. Place cuttings in warm, humid conditions until roots form.

Plants of the gray-leaved Artemisia 'Powis Castle' soften the edges of beds and borders.

ABSINTHIUM (AB-SIN-thee-um)
Absinthe, Wormwood
Color: Gray
Zones: 3 to 8

The finely divided silvery green foliage consists of 2- to 5-inch-long leaves and is evergreen and delicately fragrant. Plants can grow to 3 feet (although 2 feet is more common) and bear small gray flowers in long branched spikes. The long-outlawed beverage absinthe, made from this plant and popular in southern Europe in the nineteenth century, was found to cause delirium, hallucinations, and permanent mental illness. First manufactured by Pernod in 1797, production continued until 1939, after which the use of *A. absinthium* in the drink was discontinued. Regardless of its checkered history, plants make excellent garden specimens.

Cultivars

'Lambrook Silver' is more silvery and has a more graceful habit than the species. Plants are about 2½ feet tall and the finely divided foliage makes an excellent contrast to green-leaved plants.

LUDOVICIANA (LOO-DO-VIS-EE-AYE-NA)
Western or White Sage
Color: Gray
Zones: 4 to 9

This native species, found from California to Nebraska, is also an excellent silver- to gray-leaved species. The foliage differs from that of other species as it is not deeply divided (entire leaves); the look is clean-cut rather than busy. Plants grow 2 to 4 feet tall, are much less woody than other species, and produce grayish flowers in late summer. Plants are tolerant of warm temperatures and may be cut back without damage.

Roots ramble underground to form significant thickets. Plants may be divided in early spring or fall or propagated from terminal cuttings in spring and summer. Some of the more popular cultivars of artemisias belong to this species and may be found from Michigan to Florida.

Cultivars

'Latiloba' stands 1 to 2 feet tall and bears lovely 3-inch-wide gray-green leaves. This especially handsome cultivar makes an effective groundcover. The best of the available cultivars.

'Silver King' is cold hardy (to Zone 3) and offers excellent silver foliage. The flowering plumes turn red in the fall in northern gardens. Plants are both popular and handsome.

'Silver Queen' produces sparse female flowers and silver leaves with more deeply cut jagged margins than those of the species.

× 'POWIS CASTLE' (PO-IS)
Powis Castle Artemisia
No flowers
Zones: 6 to 8

I first came across this hybrid during a visit to Powis Castle in central Wales, whence it originated, and was much impressed with the grayness of the finely cut foliage and the low-growth habit. After a few years, I was pleasantly surprised to see plants offered in the United States. 'Powis Castle' is a hybrid between *A. arborescens* and *A. absinthium*, and blends the graceful foliage of the former with the hardiness of the latter. No flowers are produced. Plants in my garden retain their steely gray color throughout the entire growing season and have at least tripled in size. They become very woody but may be cut back if necessary. Cutting back in late fall or early spring helps retain a more refined growth habit but ultimate plant size is smaller on pruned plants. Heat hasn't bothered them, but they don't appear to be reliably cold hardy north of Zone 6, although they may come back in Zone 5 if cut back and mulched well. Propagate by cuttings only.

SCHMIDTIANA (SHMIT-EE-AYE-NA)
Silvermound Artemisia
Color: Silver-gray
Zones: 3 to 7

By far the most highly propagated species of *Artemisia* in the United States, these plants are particularly beautiful in the spring when their finely divided silver-gray foliage appears almost silky. Although the species is 2 feet tall, the most common form in nurseries is a dwarf known as 'Silver Mound', in which plants grow as compact mounds. In the landscape, plants retain this wonderful form in areas where summers are cool, but "melt out" in the center where temperatures and humidity are high. This is not a recommended landscape plant for the South, and is overpromoted and oversold. In the South, plants retain their mounded shape longer if placed in planters or other large containers, off the ground. Propagate by taking a cutting consisting of leaf, petiole, and a piece of the stem in the summer.

The deep green, variegated foliage of Arum italicum *'Pictum' are most handsome in early spring, followed by white flowers and red berries in the fall.*

ARUM (AR-um)
Arum

Approximately 12 species reside in this interesting genus, all of which are grown for their handsome cool-season foliage and naked fruit in late summer and early fall.

ITALICUM (I-TAL-I-CUM)
Italian Arum
Color: Creamy white
Zones: 5 to 9

This unique 12- to 20-inch-tall plant is used in the front of the garden as groundcover and for late-season interest. The foliage is dark lustrous green, the flowers are surrounded by a cream-colored spathe (a cloaklike structure, as in jack-in-the-pulpit), and the berries are bright orange. Propagate by division or by stratifying seed. This means that seeds are sown in a seed tray, watered well and covered with plastic and the tray is placed at 40 degrees Fahrenheit for four to six weeks. After removal from the cold, place tray at 60 degrees Fahrenheit.

Cultivars

'Marmoratum' has broad gray-green leaves with yellow and green splotches throughout—a difficult-to-locate cultivar well worth trying. Some authorities lump this cultivar with 'Pictum'. There appear, however, to be enough differences to help separate them.

'Pictum' is the best form of the species (although not the only one) whose dark green, arrowhead-shaped leaves are conspicuously blotched with gray and cream. Plants grow approximately 18 inches tall and spread slowly by tuberous roots. Clustered upright spikes of shiny orange berries appear in the fall in most areas, but I have yet to see any in my Georgia garden. Warm soil temperatures appear to inhibit fruit formation.

Bold plants of Aruncus dioicus *truly catch the eye when creamy white flowers appear in the summer.*

ARUNCUS (AH-RUN-KUS)
Goat's Beard

Plants carry male or female flowers on large, showy cream-colored panicles. I suppose they look like the beard on a goat but not any goat I have ever seen. The light green compound (like that of an ash) foliage is produced on 5- to 6-foot tall plants. The most common species is the tall *A. dioicus* (common goat's beard), but recently plants of a dwarf species, *A. aethusifolius*, have become available.

AETHUSIFOLIUS (AYE-THUS-I-FOL-EE-US)
Korean Goat's Beard
Color: Creamy white
Zones: 4 to 7
◐ ○

A terrific small species with dark green compound foliage and plumes of creamy white flowers that rise 9 to 15 inches in height. Plants in its southern range should be placed in partial shade, farther north in full sun, and provided with constant moisture. They are particularly effective in the rock garden or along a woodland path. Unfortunately, I have not been particularly successful with any species of goat's beard in north Georgia and cannot recommend plants south of Zone 7. Propagate by division or fresh seed.

DIOICUS (DIE-O-EYE-CUS)
Goat's Beard
Color: Creamy white
Zones: 4 to 7
○

This is a magnificent plant if provided dappled shade, sufficient moisture, and lots of room. Specimens can easily grow 5 feet tall and equally wide. The light green foliage beautifully combines with large plumed flower panicles. Plants are particularly handsome in the Northeast but do poorly in the South. Male and female plants occur and, if possible, the female forms should be avoided because the seed heads result in heavily laden inflorescences. Unfortunately, it is impossible to distinguish male from female plants without the presence of fruit or flowers. Reputable nurseries propagate male plants vegetatively, resulting in male offspring. Plants may be propagated by division (usually in the fall) but the root system is particularly tough. When dividing, bring your pickaxe, chainsaw, or both.

Cultivars

'Kneiffii' (NEFF-EE-EYE) has beautiful highly dissected feathery foliage and the same cream-white flowers as the species. Plants, however, are only about 3 feet tall and are more appropriate for small gardens than the species.

The handsome variegated leaves of Asarum shuttleworthii 'Callaway' cover the ground in the author's garden. Beneath the foliage are the burgundy, inflated flowers.

ASARUM (A-SAR-um)
Wild Ginger, Little Brown Jugs

Many handsome species of *Asarum* occur in nature and their popularity increases yearly. The roots of most species smell of ginger, but are not used commercially as such; the roots are edible, but seldom substituted for the real thing. Of the approximately 60 species, unfortunately fewer than half a dozen are easily available. Plants are tolerant of heavy shade and grown for their shiny, often mottled foliage. The leaves of wild ginger show a good deal of variation; most species have a mottled as well as a green form. The urn-shaped flowers are found under the leaves only if one takes the time to look. They are fascinating flowers, reminding one of the saying "a pig in a poke," and are great fun to show children and nongardening friends. You don't have to tell them that the flowers are pollinated by dirty ground-hugging bugs. Some taxonomists have split the genus into two main sections, placing the evergreen forms in *Hexastylis* and the deciduous species remaining in *Asarum*. Propagate all species by division in the spring or propagate a small section of root with a pair of leaves attached in the spring.

*CANADENSE (KAN-A-DEN-see)
Canadian Wild Ginger
Color: Purple
Zones: 4 to 8

The roots (rhizomes) are aromatic and have been used as a substitute for ginger. The somewhat hairy, kidney-shaped leaves are 4 to 6 inches across and held on long petioles (leaf stems). Native to woodlands of eastern North America, plants tolerate shade and heat and are useful for the southern and northern gardener alike. Other excellent species are A. *europaeum*, A. *speciosum*, and A. *arifolium*.

SHUTTLEWORTHII
(SHUT-TULL-WORTH-EE-EYE)
Shuttleworth's Wild Ginger
Color: Purple
Zones: 5 to 8

An evergreen member of the wild gingers, the plant is also known as *Hexastylis shuttleworthii*. The 3-inch-wide, heart-shaped-to-rounded leaves are mottled white on top and paler beneath. Plants are only 4 to 6 inches tall and spread well in rich moist soil. Flowers are mottled violet within and about 1½ inches long; push away the leaves to find them.

Cultivars

'Callaway' is more vigorous than the species and the leaves are beautifully mottled. This is one of the most visible gingers due to the white veining on the foliage. Plants were first found growing at Callaway Gardens in Pine Mountain, Georgia.

ASTER (AS-TUR)
Aster

This large genus consists of more than 600 species, many native to North America, and is being rediscovered by gardeners. The daisylike flowers of many hues may be borne singly or in inflorescences, and the alternately arranged leaves are hairy in most species. Plants range in height from less than 1 foot (*A. alpinus*) to well over 6 feet (*A. tataricus*). The taller species, such as New England aster (*A. novae-angliae*), New York aster (*A. novi-belgii*), and the Tatarian aster (*A. tataricus*) may require staking, stem thinning, or cutting back to keep the plants in check. Most species require long nights to produce flowers and bloom in the fall; however, a few (*A. alpinus*, *A.* × *frikartii*) flower in the summer. Many asters make excellent cut flowers and are presently in demand by flower arrangers and florists throughout the country. Propagate in spring or fall by division of outer portions of plant roots or take terminal cuttings in spring through summer.

The deep lavender flowers of Aster novi-belgii *'Winston S. Churchill' make a stunning display in late summer and early fall.*

ALPINUS (Al-PINE-us)

Alpine Aster

Color: Purple

Zones: 4 to 7

○

While only 6 to 9 inches tall, plants bear 1- to 2-inch-wide solitary flowers over handsome narrow leaves. They perform better in cool, rather than southern, climes and persist in the garden for three to four years only. The flowers of the species are usually purple with yellow centers but numerous cultivars are available.

Cultivars

'Dark Beauty' has dark blue, almost purple, flowers.

'Goliath' has light blue flowers 2 to 3 inches in diameter on stems 12 to 15 inches tall.

'Happy End' has rose-pink flowers on 9-inch-tall plants.

× *FRIKARTII* (FRI-KART-ee-eye)

Frikart's Aster

Color: Lavender-blue

Zones: 5 to 8

○

Plants are the result of a cross between *A. amellus* (Italian aster) and *A. thompsonii* (Thompson's aster), and were selected by Frikart's Nursery in Switzerland in 1920. It is an excellent, long-flowering hybrid; the 2-inch-wide blue flowers begin in June or early July, continue for six to eight weeks, and often rebloom in late fall. The 2- to 3-foot plants are resistant to powdery mildew, a major problem with some of our native asters.

Cultivars

'Monch' bears lavender-blue flowers and stands 2½ to 3 feet tall with a 3-foot spread. In my garden, plants tend to sprawl but flower for many weeks. This excellent plant provides pleasant blue daisies in the heat of the summer.

'Wonder of Staffa' is similar to 'Monch' but has lighter blue flowers and is slightly taller. Few differences in cultivars occur so one cannot go wrong with either of them.

NOVAE-ANGLIAE (NO-VAY-ANG-lee-aye)

New England Aster

Colors: Various

Zones: 4 to 8

○

The species, native from Quebec to South Carolina and west to Colorado, bears little resemblance to the many cultivars available from today's nurseries. They are vigorous growers, attaining heights of 4 to 6 feet, and often must be staked or supported. Place in full sun or plants will fall over. The foliage is susceptible to powdery mildew and rust and should be thinned every year. Plant in a well-ventilated area to reduce the incidence of disease. Reduce emerging stems to retain only the thickest and most vigorous. Flowers are also good as cut flowers. Plants should be divided every two to three years to maintain healthy clumps—otherwise, the clumps become too large and produce excessive foliage. Propagate by division in the spring or fall.

Cultivars

So many cultivars are available that it is impossible to include them all. The following are some of the better-known and popular ones:

'Alma Potschke' bears 1- to 2-inch-diameter rose-pink flowers on 3- to 4-foot-tall plants. A lovely cultivar with unique flower color.

'Harrington's Pink' blooms a little later than many other cultivars and produces many salmon-pink flowers on 3- to 5-foot-tall plants.

'Hella Lacy', selected by garden writer Alan Lacy and named for his wife, bears hundreds of deep purple flowers on 3-foot-tall stems.

'Purple Dome' was developed at Mt. Cuba Gardens in Delaware and is only 2 to 2½ feet tall. Plant is smothered with deep purple flowers and grows in a wonderful dome shape.

'September Ruby' is an early-flowering cultivar that begins to bloom as early as late May in the Southeast. If the flowers are removed in May, flowering occurs in late summer and fall. The deep ruby-red flowers are approximately 1 inch wide.

'Treasure' is about 4 feet tall with violet-blue flowers.

* *NOVI-BELGII*
(NO-VEE-BEL-GEE-EYE)
New York Aster, Michaelmas Aster
Colors: Various
Zones: 4 to 8
◯

From this glorious native fall-flowering weed, hundreds of cultivars have been developed that range from 5-foot-tall skyscrapers to 18-inch ground huggers. The species differs slightly from the New England aster by having smoother foliage, although with the explosion of cultivars in both species, the differences between them are somewhat blurred. Well over 300 cultivars are listed in various nursery catalogs, so there are many colors and forms of Michaelmas asters from which to choose. They provide wonderful late-summer and fall color in the garden, and are called Michaelmas daisies in the British Isles, because they bloom near September 29, St. Michael's Day.

Cultivars

Dwarf Cultivars (less than 15 inches tall)

'Audrey' has 1-inch-wide lilac flowers on 12- to 15-inch plants.

'Buxton's Blue' is only 4 to 6 inches tall and produces many small dark blue flowers.

'Jenny' (sometimes offered under *A. × dumosus*) bears red flowers on 12-inch stems.

'Prof. Kippenburg' is an excellent cultivar with lavender-blue semidouble flowers on 9- to 12-inch plants. Sometimes offered as *A. × dumosus*. One of the best low-growing asters.

'Snowsprite' has semidouble white flowers with yellow centers and is approximately 15 inches tall. Sometimes listed as *A. dumosus*.

Medium Cultivars (less than 4 feet tall)

'Ada Ballard' has double lavender-blue flowers on 3-foot-tall plants.

'Eventide' produces 1- to 2-inch wide semidouble violet-blue flowers.

'Ernest Ballard' (2 to 3 feet) has reddish pink semidouble flowers.

'Mt. Everest' has good, clear white flowers on 3-foot-tall stems.

Tall Cultivars (more than 4 feet tall)

'Climax' reaches 5 feet with large light blue flowers.

'White Ladies' is 5 to 6 feet tall and bears clear white flowers with orange-yellow centers.

TATARICUS (TA-TAR-I-CUS)
Tatarian Aster
Color: Lavender-blue
Zones: 4 to 8
○

The Tatarian aster is truly a gem for the fall garden, flowering when most other asters have given up and when late sunflowers and toad lilies need some company. The plants prefer full sun, although they flower well and are taller in partially shaded areas. The starry flowers occur in large heads atop 5- to 7-foot-tall stems in September and October. The 2-inch-long, coarse-toothed leaves resemble chard in the spring and early summer, but it is not until late summer and early fall that much happens. In the summer, however, a tremendous amount of growth occurs and before long the back of the garden is alive once more. Place with yellow sunflowers or late, red salvias for a wonderful combination. Propagate easily by division in the spring. Plants spread by underground stems and colonize an area in two to three years.

Other Species

Many excellent species of *Aster* could be incorporated in American gardens. Some include:

A. *amellus*, Italian aster, grows about 2½ feet tall and flowers in early fall. 'King George'

has deep purple flowers and is an exceptionally fine cultivar that performs better in the North than in the South.

A. divaricatus, white wood aster, tolerates dry shade and produces lovely small white flowers in September and October. Native to the eastern United States, the 1- to 2-foot-tall plant needs to be used more.

A. lateriflorus var. *horizontalis* is 2 to 4 feet tall and 4 feet wide, with lavender-purple flowers on stems arranged like horizontal stairs. Plant flowers in October and it is truly marvelous. Absolutely fabulous in Wave Hill Garden in New York.

ASTILBE (AS-TIL-BE)
Astilbe

One of the backbones of the shaded garden, few should be without a cultivar or two of *Astilbe*. Breeders from England, Germany, Switzerland,

Nestled into a sheltered shady garden, flowers of Astilbe × arendsii *'Spinell' light up a cloudy summer morning.*

and America have provided forms and colors to suit almost any taste. Although hybrids are more commonly available, numerous species have also been selected for garden use, and plants range from 12-inch-tall miniatures to 3- to 4-foot-high specimens. *Astilbe* should be placed in partially shaded, damp areas and, if not allowed to dry out, will perform admirably even in sunny locations. If allowed to dry out, however, leaves turn brown and plants are stunted with small flowers. Propagate all forms of *Astilbe* by division in the spring. Plants are large enough for division after approximately three years in one location.

× *ARENDSII*
(AH-RENDZ-ee-eye)
Hybrid Astilbe
Colors: Various
Zones: 3 to 9

The original hybrids were first selected by Lemoine Nursery in France around 1907; then, in 1920, Arend's Nursery in Germany really went to work on *Astilbe*, and these lovely hybrids continue to be developed by breeders throughout the world. The compound leaves are light green to deep bronze and many flower colors are available. Plants are generally 18 to 24 inches tall, but more vigorous cultivars may attain heights of over 3 feet. Always place in moist, partially shaded conditions; partial shade is particularly critical in the South. If plants are in a boglike area that remains moist constantly, they are more tolerant of full sun conditions. Allowing plants to dry out is the most effective means of destroying a planting. Plant in groups of at least three, more where possible. Propagate by division after three to five years.

Cultivars

Literally hundreds of cultivars have been developed and I like them all. I count 91 different species and cultivars in one catalog alone. Some are listed under various hybrid species but I lump them together as one. Here are a few of my favorites.

White Flowers

'Avalanche' is only about 18 inches tall with fine white flowers.

'Bridal Veil' bears pure white flowers on 2½- to 3-foot plants and is one of the later cultivars to flower.

'Deutschland' has clear white flowers with deep green foliage. One of the earliest to flower. Plants grow 2 to 2½ feet tall.

'Irrlicht' produces blush white flowers that age to creamy white on 2- to 3-foot plants. The deep green foliage is a lovely contrast.

'Snowdrift' has some of the cleanest white flowers in the group and is an excellent low-growing (15 inches tall) cultivar.

Pink and Rose Flowers

'Bressingham Beauty' has arching plumes of clear pink flowers on 3½-foot-tall plants.

'Cattleya' has wonderful tall spires that open rose pink and turn to lavender as they age. The 2½- to 3-foot-tall plants bear dark green foliage.

'Erica' is a medium- to late-flowering cultivar with large open plumes of pink flowers on plants 2½ to 3 feet tall.

two weeks later than those of *B. chinensis* and plants stand 18 to 24 inches tall. The clean color makes it a standout in the summer garden. Black berries are also formed but plants do not self-sow as readily as *B. chinensis*. As this excellent plant becomes more available, it should find a place in many gardens.

Cultivars

'Hello Yellow' has unspotted yellow flowers and is available from progressive nurseries— a wonderful plant.

With flowers spilling out from every inch of Boltonia asteroides 'Snowbank', *these plants resemble their name. The orange flowers at the base are* Zinnia linearis.

* *BOLTONIA* (BOWL-TONE-EE-A)
Boltonia

Many native North American plants are worthy of our gardens, and this is one of the best. The best garden species is *B. asteroides* (white boltonia), native from Connecticut to Florida and west to Louisiana.

ASTEROIDES (AS-TER-OIDE-EES)
White Boltonia
Color: White
Zones: 4 to 9
◯

The species is a little too tall for most gardens, but the selection 'Snowbank' is spectacular. The gray-green foliage is ornamental throughout the season and the sturdy, self-supporting stems grow 3 to 4 feet tall. In late summer, the plants form high mounds covered with small white daisies with yellow centers, truly like snowbanks. Plants require full sun to be at their best, although flowering will be adequate in areas of partial shade. In my Georgia garden, flowers begin to open around the fifteenth of August and continue for five weeks. Plants are tolerant of heat, humidity, and drought, and no self-respecting insect or disease organism bothers them. Need I say more? Plants are easily propagated by division in spring or fall. A single cut with a spade in the spring yields dozens of plantlets.

Other Species

Boltonia rosea is sold as a separate species but may be a rose-colored cultivar ('Rosea'). It needs full sun or is awful. The flowers are handsome but plants are not as sturdy as 'Snowbank' and tend to flop over. Propagate similar to 'Snowbank'.

The white leaf margins of Brunnera macrophylla *'Variegata' brighten shady, moist areas in a woodland garden.*

BRUNNERA (BRUNN-ER-A)
Brunnera

The genus consists of three species but only *B. macrophylla* (heartleaf brunnera) is easily available to the gardener. All species require at least partial shade and consistently moist soil.

MACROPHYLLA (MAK-RO-FIL-A)
Heartleaf Brunnera
Color: Blue
Zones: 3 to 7

Running along a shaded stream bank or meandering along the edge of a woodland—this is where *Brunnera* is happiest. Moist soil and partial shade allow plants to multiply rapidly and make an effective groundcover. If planted in too much sun, plants are stunted and foliage burns around the margins. Small blue flowers resembling forget-me-nots cascade over the developing foliage in the spring, and as the plants mature the foliage becomes larger and more heart shaped. These are lovely, understated plants when allowed to find their proper niche.

Large flowers of Campanula carpatica *var.* turbinata *cover the ground in a spring rock garden.*

Cultivars

'Hadspen Cream' has light green leaves with irregular creamy white borders.

'Langtrees' has dark green leaves with silver-white spots on the margins.

'Variegata', also sold as 'Dawson's White', is characterized by foliage with large, clean white borders and lavender-blue flowers. Although slower growing than the species, the plant is wonderfully ornamental. Plants must be divided in spring or fall to maintain ornamental foliage.

CAMPANULA
(KAM-PAHN-ew-la)
Bellflower

More than 250 species have been attributed to this genus, ranging from 4-foot giants to 4-inch midgets. Flowers are generally in shades of blue and bell shaped, but white flowers are not uncommon. All bellflowers do better in cooler climates than in the South, although some species are more heat tolerant than others. Unfortunately, many of the upright forms do not perform well in areas where summers are hot, and are not generally recommended for southern gardens. The dwarf forms are best suited for the front of the garden or rock garden and, if provided with excellent drainage, are more tolerant of heat and humidity than their taller cousins. Full sun is best for the taller species; partial shade is tolerated but not particularly beneficial for the dwarf forms. All species may be propagated by seed and terminal cuttings and division (best in spring) may also be used to multiply your plants.

CARPATICA (KAR-PA-TI-CA)
Carpathian Bellflower
Color: Blue
Zones: 3 to 8
○

Ranging in height from 6 to 12 inches, this low-growing bellflower is one of the most adaptable for American gardens. It is more tolerant of heat than many others, although good drainage is still essential. The solitary bell-shaped flowers may be up to 2 inches across and cover the plants in late spring and early summer. Plants make a terrific show the first two years, then may have to be replaced; this is particularly true in warmer areas of the country.

Cultivars

'Alba' bears white cup-shaped flowers on plants 9 inches tall.

'Blue Clips' are 6 to 9 inches tall and bear large blue flowers in the spring.

'Blue Moonlight' has bright blue flowers and is 8 to 10 inches tall. Var. *turbinata* has some of the largest flowers. Its compact, 6- to 9-inch-tall frame is covered with flowers in spring. Cultivars of this variety include 'Alba' (white), 'Karl Foerster' (light blue) and 'Pallida' (dark blue).

'Wedgewood Blue' and 'Wedgewood White' are 6 to 9 inches tall and bear violet-blue and white flowers respectively.

GLOMERATA (GLO-ME-RAH-TA)
Clustered Bellflower
Color: Dark blue
Zones: 3 to 8
○ ◐

The blossoms of this upright bellflower are clustered near the top of the stem, thus the common name. The 12- to 18-inch-tall plants are tolerant of partial shade, particularly in the South, and persist about three years before declining. Stems are excellent for cut flowers and persist up to two weeks if placed in a flower preservative solution.

Cultivars

'Crown of Snow' ('Schneekrone') bears large white flower clusters on plants 18 to 24 inches tall.

'Joan Elliott' grows about 18 inches tall and produces numerous clusters of deep violet-blue flowers.

'Superba' is one of the most vigorous cultivars, growing to 2½ feet tall. Plants bear violet flowers and appear to be more heat tolerant than others.

'Superba Alba' is the white form of the 'Superba'.

PERSICIFOLIA (PER-SIS-i-FOL-EE-A)
Peachleaf Bellflower
Colors: Various
Zones: 3 to 8

Numerous colors of peachleaf bellflower occur, including shades of blue, lavender, and white, in handsome single and wretched double flowers. Plants grow 1 to 3 feet tall and bear erect, broad bell-shaped flowers. They are excellent garden plants and even better cut flowers. Provide good drainage. Plants have enjoyed mixed reviews throughout the country. In the North they are wonderful; in the South they are difficult to establish and often disappointing.

Cultivars

'Alba' has white flowers on plants 2 to 3 feet tall.

'Beechwood' is 2 to 4 feet tall and bears pale, soft blue flowers.

'Blue Belle' has single blue flowers on stems 2 to 3 feet tall.

'Gardenia' produces many double blue flowers. Flowers don't have as "classic" a bellflower look as other bellflowers but they persist longer and are good for cut flowers. Plants are 3 to 4 feet tall.

'Telham Beauty' is 3 to 4 feet tall with bell-shaped, pale, China blue flowers. One of the most handsome bellflowers.

'Snowdrift' has large white flowers on stems 2 to 3 feet tall.

PORTENSCHLAGIANA (POR-TEN-SCHLAG-EE-AH-NA)
Dalmatian Bellflower
(syn. *C. muralis*)
Color: Blue
Zones: 4 to 8

In spite of a name that is almost unpronounceable, this wonderful dwarf bellflower scampers over walls and through rock gardens with abandon. Dalmatian bellflower is tolerant of a wide range of climates and, although the flowers are smaller than those of *C. carpatica*, plants are more heat tolerant. Plants grow 4 to 6 inches tall.

Cultivars

Var. *alba* has white flowers but is otherwise similar to the species.

'Major' has large flowers.

'Resholt Variety' bears lavender-blue flowers on plants 6 to 9 inches tall.

Other Species

Another excellent little plant suitable for walls, nooks, and crannies is *C. poscharskyana*, Serbian bellflower. Similar in habit and slightly different in flower shape, it provides a river of blue to cascade over lifeless walls and stones.

Large plants of Caryopteris × clandonensis *'Longwood Blue' thrive in the Royal Botanical Garden in Hamilton, Ontario.*

CARYOPTERIS
(KA-REE-OP-TE-RIS)
Bluebeard

Only the hybrid (*C.* × *clandonensis*) is perennial in most of the country; *C. incana* (*C.* × *bungei*), native to China and Japan, is perennial only in the Deep South. Bluebeard has become much more available and popular in recent years and the combination of blue flowers with gray-green foliage is particularly handsome.

× *CLANDONENSIS*
(KLAN-DON-EN-SIS)
Blue Mist
Color: Lavender-blue
Zones: 5 to 9
○

The hybrid, a cross between *C. incana* and *C. mongholica*, grows 3 to 4 feet tall and bears many flowers whenever a leaf attaches to the stem (leaf axil). The gray-green foliage is sufficiently ornamental for plants to be used as informal hedges and screens. Plants die to the ground in the fall but produce woody stems within a single year. A terrific plant for many uses including screening and cut flowers. Propagate by division in spring or fall or by terminal cuttings in the spring.

Cultivars

'Blue Mist' has gray-green leaves and light blue flowers.

'Heavenly Blue' has darker green leaves and darker blue flowers than the species. An excellent cultivar.

'Longwood Blue', selected at Longwood Gardens, Pennsylvania, produces silvery foliage and sky blue flowers. Plants grow 1½ to 2 feet tall.

Flowers of cupid's-dart, Catananche caerulea, *appear in the spring and remain for many weeks in sunny and partially shaded areas.*

CATANANCHE
(KAT-A-NAN-KEE)
Cupid's-Dart

This genus' claim to fame is that the plants were once used in the making of love potions; the flowers still symbolize love. Place in full sun and enjoy the flowers in fresh or dry bouquets.

CAERULEA (SE-RU-LEE-A)
Blue Cupid's-Dart
Color: Blue
Zones: 3 to 8

The 8- to 12-inch-long leaves are often gray-green, particularly when young, and hairy on both sides. The blue dandelion-like flowers sport short yellow stamens and are borne singly on 2- to 3-foot-long naked flower stems. Plants may be divided or propagated by terminal cuttings.

Cultivars

'Alba' bears white flowers, a second-rate color for cupid's-dart in my opinion.

'Bicolor' bears flowers with white petals and a dark center.

'Major' produces plants 2 to 3 feet tall with large lavender-blue flowers.

The bright yellow color of Centaurea macrocephala *is wonderful in the summer garden, and the flowers are excellent as cut flowers.*

CENTAUREA (SEN-TOR-REE-A)
Cornflower, Knapweed

A wonderful genus with marvelous species for the American gardener. Most species are upright and generally grow 2 to 3 feet tall, although 4-foot plants are not terribly uncommon. Flower heads of all species have overlapping scales immediately beneath the petals, which result in handsome flower buds as well as flowers. Cornflowers require full sun and some are better suited for the northern states due to their intolerance of hot weather. Most species are also excellent as cut flowers. Propagation by seed is most effective but plants may also be divided carefully in the spring.

DEALBATA (DEEL-BAH-TA)
Persian Cornflower
Color: Lavender-rose
Zones: 3 to 7

The 2- to 3-inch-diameter solitary, fringed flower heads open in late spring to early summer.

Three- to 4-foot plants have lobed foliage with long hairs on the underside providing a whitish appearance. In north Georgia, plants tend to flop more than in northern states and can't be recommended for areas with warm, humid summers.

Cultivars

'Sternbergii' bears rosy flowers with white centers. More compact than the species, this is a better choice for the garden.

MACROCEPHALA (MAK-RO-CEF-A-LA)
Armenian Basket Flower
Color: Yellow
Zones: 3 to 7
○

Certainly one of the most ornamental cornflowers, this 3- to 4-foot-tall plant bears bright yellow shaggy flowers and long green leaves. A marvelous plant for the rear of the flower garden, it is excellent for cut flowers; stems should be cut just as the yellow color appears, for long-lasting cuttings. Unfortunately, plants are not particularly tolerant of warm summers and I don't grow it in my north Georgia garden. However, in the Midwest and North, plants are wonderful. This is a plant whose bold coarseness is an asset.

MONTANA (MON-TAH-NA)
Mountain Bluet
Color: Deep blue
Zones: 3 to 8
○ ◑

The flowers have a reddish center and the tips of the petals are divided into three to five short segments each. The flowers also sport handsome scales at their bases. Plants are 1½ to 2 feet tall and can move swiftly through the garden. In the

North they are a weed, albeit a pretty one, taking over with abandon. In the South they are better behaved. Place in full sun and let them roam; if partial shade is provided, plants roam equally freely but are taller and bear fewer flowers.

Cultivars

'Alba' has creamy white, fringed flowers (a lovely contrast to the foliage, but flowers are not white enough for my taste).

'Carnea' bears rose-pink flowers. Sometimes listed as 'Rosea'.

'Violetta' provides amethyst flowers and is a pleasant change from the species.

Falling over rocks and streaming through rock gardens, Cerastium tomentosum *provides unbeatable color in the spring garden.*

CERASTIUM (SER-ASS-TEE-UM)
Snow-in-Summer

Numerous low-growing species occur in the genus, the one of greatest importance to the American garden being common snow-in-summer, *C. tomentosum.* Plants are invasive, but still wonderfully handsome when well grown. Propagate by seed collected in the summer or by divisions in spring or fall.

TOMENTOSUM (TO-MEN-TOE-SUM)
Common Snow-in-Summer
Color: White
Zones: 2 to 7

What a marvelous sight when these 6- to 8-inch-tall plants are in full flower. Without a doubt, when grown well, plants do resemble "snow in summer" (actually snow in spring for most American gardens). Place in full sun in the North, partial shade in the South, and provide excellent drainage. Poor drainage is the main reason for "melting out" problems, and plants are not very tolerant of hot, humid summers. After flowering, take your Lawn Boy and give them a haircut; the new foliage that grows in will be more resistant to the hot weather ahead.

Cultivars

'Columnae' is less invasive than the species and more compact.

'Silver Carpet' is more matted and more compact than the species.

'Yo-Yo' has clear white flowers and is also compact and less invasive.

In full sun or in partial shade, Ceratostigma plumbagi-noides *never fails to perform or impress.*

CERATOSTIGMA
(SER - AT - O - STIG - MA)
Leadwort

Only seven or eight species occur in the genus, but the ground-hugging common leadwort, *P. plumbaginoides,* makes an excellent late-flowering groundcover.

PLUMBAGINOIDES
(PLUM - BAH - GI - NOI - DEEZ)
Common Leadwort
Color: Deep gentian blue
Zones: 5 to 9

◯

Growing 9 to 12 inches tall and bearing small flowers in summer and fall, this groundcover can

be grown equally well in Columbus, Ohio, and in Athens, Georgia. The foliage turns bronze-red with the onset of cool weather and is handsome by itself. Plants are long-lived; those in the gardens at the University of Georgia have performed well for more than five years and show no signs of decline. Flowers begin in July or August and continue through October. Propagate by cuttings or division in spring or fall. Seed germinates more readily if placed in a moist medium (sand, potting soil) and cooled at 40 degrees Fahrenheit for four to six weeks. After cooling, place seed tray at 65 to 70 degrees Fahrenheit and maintain moisture.

*CHELONE (CHEL-O-NEE)
Turtle-Head

This North American genus contains about four species, although I keep waiting for that special inspiration that suddenly will help me see any resemblance to the head of a turtle. If placed in the proper environment, plants make a lovely display in late August and September. In general, they prefer full sun in the North, partial shade in the South, and relatively moist soil conditions. Propagate by seed or division in the spring or after flowering. For best results with seed, sow in a seed tray containing a moist 1-to-1 ratio of peat and perlite or peat and vermiculite and place at 40 degrees Fahrenheit for four to six weeks. Bring out the tray and put in an area of 60 degrees Fahrenheit for germination. Terminal cuttings may also be used.

Flowering in late summer and early fall, Chelone obliqua *plants are tough but handsome in the sunny garden.*

*OBLIQUA (O-BLEE-KWA)
Rose Turtle-Head
Color: Rosy red
Zones: 5 to 8

The more I see this plant, the more I am taken by its understated charm and relative ease of culture. Although native to the mountains of the eastern United States, these 2- to 3-foot-tall plants are handsome in the gardens of southern Ontario as well as those of Charlotte, North Carolina. In fact, one of the most spectacular plantings I have seen was in early September in the Royal Botanical Gardens in Hamilton, Ontario. Growing among *Rudbeckia* and *Sedum*, plants shone like rosy beacons in the late afternoon sun. Plants make a large clump within three years if sufficient moisture is supplied. If plants constantly dry out, performance is disappointing. If planted in the South, moisture is not only beneficial, it is essential. I have grown this in our cut-flower trials at the University of Georgia and am very impressed with its heat tolerance and flowering.

Peeking out of a clump of artemisia, flowers of Chrysanthemum pacificum *appear in September and October in the Delaware garden of John and Jean Frett.*

CHRYSANTHEMUM
(KRIS-ANTH-E-MUM)
Chrysanthemum

A large genus, *Chrysanthemum* contains such well-known plants as the florist chrysanthemum and the ubiquitous hardy mum (*C. × morifolium*), ox-eye daisy (*C. leucanthemum*), feverfew (*C. parthenium*), and the lovely marguerite daisy (*C. frutescens*). Some of the best-loved and most handsome garden plants belong to other species, such as the Nippon daisy, the Japanese daisy, and our old favorite, the Shasta daisy. The nomenclature of *Chrysanthemum* has gone through some significant changes recently, with many species being split into different genera. In fact, according to recent taxonomic changes, the genus *Chrysanthemum* barely exists and should be reorganized under eight to ten different genera. Such are the complexities of taxonomy. However, a mum is still a mum and I love to make new friends and reacquaint myself with old ones. All species should be planted in full sun and require little more than adequate drainage to thrive. Propagate by division in the spring or fall or by terminal cuttings anytime.

× MORIFOLIUM
(MORE-I-FO-lee-um)
(syn. *Dendrathema grandiflora*)
Hardy Mums
Colors: Various
Zones: 3 to 10
○

Hardy mums are the ubiquitous fall mum, sold in large containers in the garden center as well as in 4-inch pots that bake on the pavement at mass retailers. Remember three things when growing hardy mums. First, they require full sun and well-drained soils; second, they should be cut back until approximately August 15 (South) or August 1 (North). Do not allow them to flower in the spring or summer. Last, do not plant until at least the middle of September, even though plants will be staring at you from every outlet long before that. This is critical in the South but is recommended everywhere. As long as chrysanthemums are well managed, they will fill in an area and become a wonderful part of the fall landscape.

NIPPONICUM (NI-PON-I-cum)
(syn. *Nipponanthemum nipponicum*)
Nippon Daisy
Color: White
Zones: 5 to 9
○

While many chrysanthemums flower in late summer and fall, the Nippon daisy flowers as late as November in protected sites. The large white Shasta-like flowers tolerate mild frosts and are wonderful for late fall. Pinch plants two or three times during the growing season, but no later than July 15, to encourage branching and floriferousness. This plant is underused in American gardens. Plants do not require division, and propagation should be accomplished by terminal cuttings.

PACIFICUM (PA-SI-FI-CUM)
(syn. *Ajania pacifica*)
Silver and Gold
Color: Yellow
Zones: 5 to 9

Although this is another very late-flowering species, the plants should be grown more for their variegated foliage than for their small, ball-like bright yellow flowers. The foliage is light green with yellow margins and is particularly handsome in the front of the garden interwoven with such gray foliage plants as *Artemisia* 'Powis Castle'. The flower buds occur from September to October and the yellow flowers appear to be imprisoned within the buds, never being more than secondary features to the fine foliage. Nevertheless, bets are taken every year to see if the flowers will color before a hard frost visits. When they do, they surely add interest to the fall garden. If placed in partial shade, leaves may expand more than in full sun but flowers may not appear. Reports of poor overwintering have plagued this species since its inception, more likely due to poor drainage than poor cold tolerance. Good drainage is essential for these plants; they are not winter hardy if the roots are awash in winter moisture. Propagate by terminal cuttings in spring or summer.

× SUPERBUM (SOO-PERB-um)
Shasta Daisy
Colors: Various
Zones: 4 to 9

Few gardens are without a Shasta daisy or two, a legacy from one of our finest plantsmen, Luther Burbank, who hybridized Shasta daisies in the late 1800s. The many cultivars available today are a testament to the fine breeding efforts by nurserymen in this country and abroad, and to

the plant's handsome display and ease of culture. Flowers are mostly white to creamy yellow and appear in early to midsummer, although late cultivars are presently being selected. Plants generally grow 2 to 2½ feet tall. Once flowering is complete, remove flower heads; in some cultivars, secondary flowering may occur. Unfortunately, Shastas are susceptible to numerous foliar diseases and insects and the leaves tend to look shabby after flowering. Spraying with a multipurpose fungicide reduces the incidence of many foliar diseases. To be up-to-date with the latest taxonomic efforts, readers should know that *C. × superbum* is now correctly listed as *Leucanthemum × superbum*.

Cultivars

Single Flowers

'Alaska' grows 2 to 3 feet tall and bears white flowers with yellow centers. A tried-and-true cultivar.

'Lyndsey Dawn' bears 2- to 3-inch flowers with green centers and grows about 3 feet tall.

'Polaris' has been around for many years and bears extra-large flowers on plants 3 feet tall. If wind is a problem, plants will likely require staking.

'Snowcap' is 18 inches to 2 feet tall, with many white flowers. It's particularly weather resistant and useful for smaller gardens.

'Snow Lady' is an excellent dwarf (1 to 2 feet tall), seed-propagated selection. An All-American award winner in 1988, it bears lovely white flowers with yellow centers. Very floriferous and easy to grow.

Double Flowers

'Aglaya' ('Aglaia') has fringed white petals that appear to be in need of a hairbrush. Plants are 2 to 2½ feet tall.

'Cobham Gold' bears flowers with yellow raised centers and creamy white petals on plants 1½ to 2 feet tall.

'Marconi' has large clear white flowers on 2-foot-tall stems.

'Mount Shasta', 1 to 2 feet tall, has fully double flowers surrounding a raised center.

'Thomas Killin' bears two rows of petals around a crested center. This plant is 2 to 3 feet tall and floriferous.

'Wirral Pride' bears semidouble flowers with ruffled petals on 2-foot-tall plants.

'Wirral Supreme' has large crested flowers and is very vigorous. Plants are 2 to 3 feet tall.

* *CHRYSOGONUM* (KRIS-OG-O-NUM)
Green and Gold

Another wonderful American native, plants of *C. virginianum* are found from Pennsylvania to Florida and west to Louisiana. Although the common name, green and gold, is not particularly creative, it is certainly most descriptive. Many catalogs claim that the plants flower for two months or longer. In reality, the daisylike yellow flowers are produced heavily in the spring, for about four weeks, over dark green foliage. Plants are about 6 inches tall and perform best as a groundcover in moist, shady areas. It is reliable in Zones 5 (4 with protection) to 9; I have seen beautiful plantings of green and gold from Boston to Denver and look forward to it every year in my garden in Georgia. There are other plants more flashy, but few that more reliably light up the spring garden. Propagate by division in the spring. Seeds sown in warm, moist conditions germinate in approximately two to three weeks.

The early spring woodland garden is alight with the yellow flowers of Chrysogonum virginianum.

Cultivars

A few of our more colorful nurserymen have been immortalized with recent introductions of the species.

'Alan Bush', the plant, is 4 to 8 inches tall and is a selection of var. *virginianum*. It has lighter green leaves and larger, more upright flowers than 'Martin Viette'. Named after Alan Bush, nurseryman of Holbrook Farms, Fletcher North Carolina.

'Martin Viette' (again, the plant) is only 2 to 4 inches tall with smaller, less persistent flowers than the species and dark green leaves. This is likely a selection from var. *australe*. Named for Martin Viette of Viette Nurseries, Virginia.

The purple foliage of Cimicifuga ramosa *'Brunette' contrasts beautifully with the white flowers and with other green-leaved plants in the garden.*

CIMICIFUGA
(SIM-ME-SIF-FYOU-GA)
Bugbane

If I could have every selection of *Cimicifuga* in my garden, I would find room. Alas, my patch of north Georgia clay is a little too warm for good performance of most of the bugbanes. In general, plants produce tall candlelike spires of white flowers in late summer and fall and are most effective north of Zone 7. *Cimicifuga americana* may be found in shady, moist areas as far south as Atlanta, Georgia. All species have compound leaves and perform well in moist, partially shaded areas with a good supply of organic matter. The beauty of the flowers comes from their long stamens; little color or form can be credited to the small, often nonexistent petals. Plants combine beautifully with the fall-flowering anemones and salvias. Propagation by seed is difficult. If possible, collect fresh seed, sow in a well-drained medium and place outdoors in a cold frame or under snow cover for the winter. Germination is erratic and seedlings may not emerge for as long as 12 months. Root cuttings may also be used, but propagation of *Cimicifuga* is best left to the nurseryman.

RAMOSA (RAY-MOE-SA)
Branched Bugbane
Color: White
Zones: 3 to 7

Although not yet as common in American gardens as other species, it is becoming the species of choice. Many long, dense flower spikes appear on 5- to 7-foot-tall plants during late summer and fall. Native to Japan, plants have found their way into this country, and recent selections have made them particularly attractive for the late-flowering garden.

Cultivars

Var. *atropurpurea* is 4 to 7 feet tall and has purplish foliage flushed with green. The dark foliage contrasts well with the white spires.

'Brunette' is shorter (3 to 4 feet) and has stunning purple foliage. The foliage does not appear to fade during the summer; this is a truly outstanding garden plant.

SIMPLEX (SIM-PLEX)
Kamchatka Bugbane
Color: White
Zones: 3 to 8

I include this native Russian plant because of its combination of arching flowers and tolerance to cold and heat. The long white spires arch gracefully and are softer in appearance than the stiffer spikes of other species. This is the latest bugbane to flower, often flowering right through the first frost. The late-flowering aspect is useful but Kamchatka bugbane is also one of the most heat-tolerant species I have tried. Although not yet content in my Georgia garden, plants have outperformed other unhappy species and selections planted alongside them there.

Cultivars

'Elstead Variety' has finely cut dark foliage and purplish brown flower buds that give rise to long white flowers.

'White Pearl' has performed remarkably well in my garden, producing fat white flower spires in early to mid-October and persisting until the first week of November. One of the more heat-tolerant cultivars I have tested.

Clematis integrifolia, *a nonclimbing clematis, forms a lovely clump in this Philadelphia garden.*

CLEMATIS (KLEM-A-TIS)
Clematis

Although best known for the wonderful flowering vines (*C.* × *jackmanii,* × *durandii, montana,* 'Nelly Moser' and so on) that spill over walls and trellises and decorate mailboxes, *Clematis* also contains a few handsome nonvining members. All prefer full sun but tolerate afternoon shade.

HERACLEIFOLIA
(HE-RA-KLEE-I-FO-LEE-A)
Tube Clematis
Color: Blue
Zones: 3 to 7

The dark green compound leaves consist of 3 to 5 pointed leaflets. The tube-like flowers have no petals, the sepals being responsible for the hyacinth blue color. About 6 to 12 blooms appear in each flower cluster from late spring to late summer, depending on the area of the country, and then give way to handsome fluffy seed heads. Plants are vigorous growers, particularly in areas of mild summers, and may flop over if not supported.

Cultivars

'Côte d'Azur' has lighter blue flowers than the species.

'Wyevale Blue' bears darker blue flowers than the species.

INTEGRIFOLIA
(IN-TEG-RI-FO-LEE-A)
Solitary Clematis
Color: Indigo-violet
Zones: 3 to 7
○

Indigo-violet single flowers appear in the summer at the ends of the stems. They are at their most handsome when the urn-shaped flowers turn up their sepals in early summer. Like other species, this plant produces ornamental fluffy seed heads after flowering. Heat tolerance is not as good as in *heracleifolia*, and this species should not be grown much south of Zone 7. Some of the finest plants I have seen are grown in the Philadelphia area. Support plants as needed. Not as vigorous as *C. heracleifolia*.

Cultivars

'Hendersonii' has dark blue flowers and is a most popular selection.

'Rosea' bears rose-colored flowers.

Lily-of-the-valley, Convallaria majalis, *overruns the rocks and paths in the spring landscape.*

CONVALLARIA
(KON-VAL-AIR-ee-A)
Lily of the Valley

Growing up in Montreal, where lily of the valley (*C. majalis*) grew rampant, I cursed the stuff whenever I had to keep it in bounds in the garden. I pulled, I yanked, and I dug, knowing full well that more would eventually appear. Now that I live in Georgia, I find I miss it enormously. I caress and care for it here as if it was an award-winning rose because now I must go north to see grand plantings of this fragrant weed. Such are the vicissitudes of life!

The flowers are small, white and wonderfully fragrant. A few plants by themselves are handsome, but this is best used as a groundcover. They grow only 12 inches tall and are vigorous in Zones 2 to 7. The vigor of the underground stems makes these plants particularly valuable for filling in large areas in a rock garden or along sides of paths. Plants look best when cuddled around ornamental rocks. Place in full sun in the North or in partial shade in the South. Propagation is easy: simply take a strong shovel and rip up a bunch of roots. Split into individual "pips" and replant immediately.

Cultivars

'Albistriata', also listed as 'Striata' and 'Variegata', has beautiful dark green leaves with yellow striations. Not as vigorous as the species but the foliage certainly adds a new dimension to the spring garden. Unfortunately, new green foliage without striations tends to appear; it should be ruthlessly extracted.

'Fortin's Giant' has larger flowers and is the cultivar of choice, if available.

'Rosea' bears light pink to rose-colored flowers. It is not as vigorous or floriferous as the species.

* *COREOPSIS* (KO-REE-OP-SIS)
Tickseed

Coreopsis consists of more than 100 species, and many are mainstays of the garden. Flowering from early spring to late summer, they are some of the most useful of plants. Full sun and well-drained sites are preferred. The daisylike flowers may be single, semidouble, or fully double, and although yellow is the dominant color of the genus, rose and bicolors are available. The name *Coreopsis* translates "like a bug," and the ticklike seeds are responsible for the common name above. Propagate by seed or terminal cuttings.

Even my old solemn frog brightens up with the bright flowers of Coreopsis auriculata *'Nana'.*

AURICULATA (OW-RIK-EW-LAH-TA)

Mouse-Ear Coreopsis
Color: Yellow
Zones: 4 to 9
◯

This spring-flowering species is represented by the dwarf cultivar 'Nana', and is one of the loveliest species in the genus. The dark green foliage stays bunched around the base and, when not in flower, plants are about 9 inches tall. The bright yellow 1- to 2-inch-diameter daisies are borne on stems 8 to 12 inches tall and light up the garden in early spring. Plants may be in flower four to six weeks. Place near the front of the garden where they can be enjoyed.

Cultivars

'Superba' can sometimes be found, and is taller with larger flowers than 'Nana', but not as handsome.

GRANDIFLORA (GRAN-DI-FLO-RA)

Tickseed
Color: Yellow and orange
Zones: 5 to 9
◯

One of the mainstays of the summer garden, this species is so successful that old-time gardeners tend to avoid it for fear of its being too common. Starting in midsummer, yellow to orange flowers appear for eight to ten weeks (if properly maintained). The spent flowers must be removed if plants are to continue blooming all summer. This is one of the highest maintenance plants, not recommended for the "low-maintenance" garden. If spent flower heads are not removed, plants rapidly become tired and explode into fiery balls of orange flowers, quickly degenerating into ugly brown seed heads. Not a pretty sight! Plants are

not long lasting and should be replaced every two or three years for best display. Some excellent cultivars are available that outshine the species in every category.

Cultivars

'Early Sunrise' is exceptional, flowering the first year from seed and providing an excellent display of bright double flowers all summer. An All-American award winner for 1989.

'Goldfink' bears 2-inch-wide golden yellow single flowers with orange centers. Just 9 inches tall, this plant is most useful at the front of the garden or tucked around rocks.

'Sunray' produces 2-inch-wide double flowers for 8 to 12 weeks and grows 2 feet tall.

VERTICILLATA (VER-TI-SI-LAH-TA)

Threadleaf Coreopsis
Color: Yellow
Zones: 3 to 9
◯

This is the most popular species, with a following of beginning and veteran gardeners alike. The threadlike leaves make it a good plant for southern gardens because they don't lose much water during the heat, an important drought-tolerant characteristic. The single yellow flowers are borne well above foliage in mid- to late summer.

Cultivars

'Grandiflora' is larger in every way than the species. The yellow flowers are up to 2½ inches wide, and plants are vigorous and fast growing.

PURPUREA (PUR-PEWR-EE-A)
Common Foxglove
Colors: Various
Zones: 3 to 8

◑

It's not a true perennial, but how can I not include such magnificent spires? Easy to propagate and grow, plants produce a symphony of color from Edmonton to Jacksonville. In warm climates plants often self-sow, but usually plants are raised from seed and placed in the garden in the fall. Winter cold is necessary to make the plants flower; therefore, if planted in the spring, no flowering will occur until one year later. Many cultivars are available, most from seed, and white ('Alba') and mixed strains (Foxy hybrids and Excelsior hybrids) are all excellent.

A wonderful plant, Echinacea purpurea 'Bright Star' is a little more compact and shorter than the native species.

** ECHINACEA* (EK-IN-AY-SEE-A)
Purple Coneflower

Approximately three species occur in this genus, but the most satisfying is *E. purpurea*, purple coneflower. Native to the central United States, this native wildflower has become established in gardens throughout the country (Zones 3 to 8). Flower stems rise 3 feet high and sport purple petals surrounding a raised tan-brown center cone in midsummer. Plants are tough, persist for many years, and tolerate partial shade but prefer full sun. If grown in too much shade, plants tend to topple and require staking. Plants should not be heavily fertilized for the same reason. An excellent cut flower, the daisies can be used in the home as is or the petals may be stripped from the center cone and the naked, globelike raised cone can be used as a long-lasting dry flower. Propagate from seed in warm, humid conditions.

Cultivars

'Abendsonne' has lighter, more cerise-pink flowers than the species.

'Bright Star' is a rose-colored, free-flowering cultivar with 2- to 3-inch-diameter flowers. Plants are seed propagated, and significant variation exists.

'Dwarf Star', a smaller version of 'Bright Star', has a dwarf stature that makes it more useful than the species for smaller gardens.

'Magnus' bears rose petals with a tan center cone. The petals are more upright than those of the species.

'Ovation' produces large rosy pink, drooping petals around a tan center cone.

'Robert Bloom' bears 4- to 5-inch-diameter, purple-rose flowers on stems 3 feet tall.

'White Lustre' has large clean white flowers with orange center cones.

'White Swan' is more dwarf (1 to 2 feet tall) than other white cultivars and bears outward-facing white petals around an orange-bronze center cone. This is the finest white cultivar available.

Loved by gardeners and passionately pursued by honeybees, the globes of Echinops bannaticus *'Taplow Blue' provide a palette of blue in the summer.*

ECHINOPS (EK-IN-OPS)
Globe Thistle

Small blue summer flowers are bundled together in round balls on tall naked stems in each of the 75 species that make up the genus. Some of the species are particularly spiny and can all but eat unwary gardeners. Common globe thistle (*E. ritro*), however, is better behaved and more handsome. Although native to Europe and western Asia, plants perform well in Zones 3 to 8. The leaves are gray-green on the underside and not at all thistly. The 1- to 2-inch-diameter blue globes form in summer and persist for six to eight weeks. Flowers are deeper blue in the North than the South due to cooler summer nights. Flowers, excellent as cut flowers, persist for 7 to 10 days in the garden and may be dried without difficulty. They also are particularly attractive to bees in the gardens. Propagate by seed or root cuttings.

Cultivars

'Blue Globe' has large silvery blue flower heads and is a slight improvement on 'Taplow Blue'. Possibly a cultivar of *E. bannaticus*.

'Taplow Blue' is the most commonly offered cultivar and may be a cultivar of *E. bannaticus*. It grows 2 to 3 feet tall and produces dozens of blue flowers.

'Veitch's Blue' has darker, steel blue flowers than either 'Taplow Blue' or the species.

The flowers of most epimediums are showy, but few are as early and handsome as those of Epimedium × versicolor *'Sulphureum'.*

EPIMEDIUM
(EP-EE-MEE-dee-um)
Barrenwort

This tall (6 to 12 inches) groundcover bears spurred flowers of white, rose, and yellow through handsome foliage and is becoming more popular every year. I like using barrenwort under my oak trees where many other species cannot grow. They are relatively slow growing but make a wonderful floral display in the spring. The foliage remains attractive throughout the season. Although epimediums tolerate warm, dry conditions, they are too special to be relegated to the poorest parts of the garden. Plant them in partial shade and moist conditions where they can grow to their fullest potential.

ALPINUM (AL-PINE-um)

Alpine Barrenwort
Colors: Red and yellow
Zones: 3 to 8

The 2- to 3-inch-long leaves, arranged in groups of three, are pointed at the end. The outer sepals are grayish with specks of red; the inner sepals are dark red, while the petals are yellowish. Plants are beautiful growing through 'April Tears' and other daffodils.

Cultivars

'Rubrum' has bright red inner sepals and brighter yellow petals than the species.

× RUBRUM (REW-brum)

Red Barrenwort
Color: Red
Zones: 4 to 8

Probably the best of the available barrenworts, plants bear large red-tinged leaves and crimson-red flowers. Plants are vigorous and grow faster than most other species. They flower in March in my garden and in April and May in the Boston area. One of the finest plantings of red barrenwort is at Garden in the Woods near Framingham, Massachusetts.

× YOUNGIANUM (YUN-GEE-AYE-NUM)

Young's Barrenwort
Colors: White, pink
Zones: 5 to 8

A hybrid of *E. diphyllum* and *E. grandiflorum*, plants bear leaves divided into nine pointed leaflets. The small pendulous white flowers are flushed with tinges of pink. The leaves emerge with a delicate red hue and turn a lovely shade of red in the fall.

Cultivars

'Niveum' ('Album') is the most common cultivar with clear white flowers.

'Roseum' ('Lilacinum') has rose-lilac flowers.

Other Species

Other excellent species of barrenwort are becoming more available and should be incorporated where possible. *E. grandiflorum* (longspur barrenwort) has spectacular flowers consisting of white outer sepals and pale yellow inner ones. 'Rose Queen' has large rose-pink flowers with white-tipped spurs. 'White Queen' has silvery white flowers.

E. × versicolor (bicolor barrenwort) is usually offered as 'Sulphureum' with flowers in shades of bright and pale yellow. It is the earliest-flowering epimedium of the many I have tried, flowering at least three weeks earlier than *E. grandiflorum* and *E. × rubrum*.

The metallic blue bracts of Eryngium alpinum *take on a ghostly blue-gray tint in the late afternoon sun.*

ERYNGIUM (E-RINJ-EE-UM)
Sea Holly

Sea holly provides some of the finest architectural plants in the perennial plant cupboard. The flowers are held in oblong or round heads surrounded by bracts, and the whole flower head is held well above the lobed, slightly spiny foliage. The flower heads turn blue as they mature, and color intensifies in areas where night temperatures stay below 70 degrees Fahrenheit. Of the hundred or so species, about half a dozen are used extensively in Europe but only two or three are seen in the United States. *E. giganteum* is a handsome biennial species with silvery blue flowers on compact plants.

ALPINUM (Al-PINE-um)
Alpine Sea Holly
Color: Metallic blue
Zones: 4 to 7
○

Some of the largest flowers in the genus are found on this species. The upper portion of the stems and the flower heads (shaped like small pineapples) turn deep blue in the summer. Plants are about 2 feet tall and bear dark green heart-shaped leaves. This species provides the most spectacular "flower power" of all the species.

Cultivars

'Amethyst' is 2 to 3 feet tall with metallic lavender flowers.

'Blue Star' has deep blue flowers on stems 2½ to 3 feet tall.

'Superbum' has some of the larger flowers in the species and can grow to 3 feet tall.

AMETHYSTINUM (A-ME-THIST-EYE-NUM)
Amethyst Sea Holly
Color: Metallic blue
Zones: 2 to 8
○

The claim to fame for this species is its cold hardiness and steely blue flower heads. The stems branch near the top and form many small (½-inch-long) flowers and long, sharply pointed bracts. The basal leaves are deeply divided, and the large bracts, blue stems, and divided foliage add a good deal of interest to the garden.

The bright yellow bracts of Euphorbia epithymoides *almost make the foliage disappear.*

EUPHORBIA (YEW-FOR-BEE-A) Spurge

This large genus contains more than a thousand species, and with that number from which to choose, surely some plants are useful for gardens. The flowers are small and the beauty of the genus results from colored bracts. Unfortunately, only four or five species are available through retail and mail-order outlets and even some of those are not always easy to find. All species produce a milky sap, which becomes a problem when stems are cut to bring indoors. Immersing freshly cut stems in hot water or diluted rubbing alcohol inhibits sap leakage.

EPITHYMOIDES (E-PI-THI-MOI-DEEZ)
(syn. *E. polychroma*)
Cushion Spurge
Color: Yellow
Zones: 4 to 8
○ ◑

I have seen wonderful specimens of this plant, in gardens from Georgia to Ohio, in which the yellow bracts cover the plant like a tablecloth. At their worst, plants can become open and somewhat scraggly as hot weather approaches. This is especially true with older plants in the southern areas of the country. Plants are rather short-lived and should be replaced every three or four years. The light green foliage is attractive, the bracts small but showy, and, overall, the plants provide a handsome spring accent. Place in partial shade in well-drained soil. Propagate from seed or 2- to 3-inch-long terminal cuttings taken after flowering is completed.

Cultivars

'Senior' bears deep yellow flowers on vigorously growing 2- to 3-foot-tall plants.

MYRSINITES (MUR-SIN-EE-TEEZ)
Myrtle Spurge
Color: Yellow
Zones: 4 to 9

The tightly wound gray-green leaves have no petioles and are pressed close to the low-lying stems along their entire length. The plants are less than 1 foot tall but put out long stems that end in bright yellow bracts. The foliage color is an excellent contrast to the bracts, which appear about the same time as daffodils. White daffodils and myrtle spurge make excellent garden companions. Plants, well adapted to warm areas, should be placed in partial shade. Propagate by seeds and cuttings.

Related Species

E. griffithii (Griffith's spurge) can be stunning and is represented by the cultivars 'Dixter' and 'Fireglow'; the species itself is seldom sold. Plants perform well in northern states but do poorly where summer temperatures are consistently high. The 2- to 3-foot-tall upright plants bear many brick red bracts over lancelike leaves. Plants prefer full sun in the North, but partial shade helps if grown south of Zone 6.

The fluffy flowers of Filipendula purpurea *are a rose color, but soon turn shades of deep purple.*

FILIPENDULA (FIL-I-PEN-DEW-LA)
Meadowsweet

The genus contains a number of species with handsome foliage and white-to-purple flowers. All are relatively cold tolerant and may be grown into northern Ontario. Many tiny flowers are held in dense flower heads in midsummer. Moisture is necessary for most species; plants do not tolerate drought particularly well.

PALMATA (PAHL-MAY-TA)
Siberian Meadowsweet
Colors: Pink and white
Zones: 3 to 8

This has always been one of my favorite garden plants, and even though it has spent eight years in my garden, I have little desire to remove it. The dark green palmate foliage (like a hand spread open) remains attractive all season if not allowed to dry out—otherwise, the margins turn brown and crinkly. In late spring or early summer, the pastel pink flower heads are formed on plants 3 to 4 feet tall, and they are transformed to a creamy white as they mature. Far more colorful plants occur, but Siberian meadowsweet provides a quiet charm at a time of year when everything seems to be competing for attention. Two problems exist, however, which cannot be ignored. First, the flowers persist for only a week or two, making the foliage even more important. While the flowers have a beauty of their own, their lack of persistence is of concern to some gardeners. Second, Japanese beetles eat it with relish and must be controlled if such pests are prevalent in your area. If beetles leave you with tattered leaves, cut back the foliage in midsummer after their feeding is complete. I bought a Japanese-beetle trap one year and attracted all the beetles from everyone else's garden. Unfortunately, each beetle ate its fill of meadowsweet before falling to its sweet demise.

Cultivars

'Alba' bears creamy white flowers.

'Digitata Nana' ('Nana') is similar to the species but grows only 8 to 12 inches tall. A lovely plant for the front of the garden.

'Elegantissima' ('Elegans') is more compact than the species and bears white flowers with pink stamens. More beautiful than the species and one of my favorites.

'Rubra' has darker flowers than the species.

PURPUREA (PUR-PUR-EE-A)
Japanese Meadowsweet
Color: Purple
Zones: 4 to 8

One of the brilliant-flowered meadowsweets, these deep purple flowers certainly brighten up the late spring and early summer garden. The large clumps produce leafy stems above which are formed flat heads of cherry red flowers. The 2- to 3-foot-tall plants require moist conditions; although they will grow in a boggy soil, they tolerate other garden conditions as long as sufficient moisture is provided. Plants are shorter where water is not constantly available. Flowers are brighter in areas of cool night temperatures than in areas where nights seldom fall below 70 degrees Fahrenheit.

VULGARIS (VUL-GAH-RIS)
(syn. *F. hexapetala*)
Dropwort
Color: White
Zones: 3 to 8

The most common meadowsweet, produces creamy white flowers often tinged with pink, borne in many 4- to 6-inch-wide flattened inflorescences. The finely divided leaves result in fernlike plants, much less coarse than *F. purpurea* and *F. palmata*. They prefer constant moisture but are more drought tolerant than other species.

Cultivars

'Flore-pleno' is a common double-flowered form, about 12 inches tall, and is particularly ornamental.

'Rosea' bears rosy pink flowers but is otherwise similar to the species.

'John Elsley', named for the fine horticulturist at Wayside Gardens, SC, bears magenta flowers over plants 9 to 12 inches high.

'Shepard's Warning' is only 4 to 6 inches tall with deep rose-pink flowers. Lovely for the rock garden but tends to get smothered in the border.

Var. *striatum* is a wonderfully handsome variety. The flowers are variable but usually appear a light pink with crimson veins. This is often sold as 'Lancastriense' or 'Prostratum' and is the best cultivar.

SYLVATICUM (SIL-VA-TI-CUM)
Wood Cranesbill
Color: Violet-blue
Zones: 5 to 8
○

One of the earliest to flower and most tolerant of shade, wood cranesbill bears small flowers and seed capsules pointing to the sky. In my garden, they flower as early as late April, in the North they flower two to four weeks later. They have more of a woodland "feel" than most other species. Propagate by seed.

Cultivars

'Album' has white flowers with light green leaves. This cultivar performed remarkably well in my shady, warm garden.

'Mayflower' bears rich violet-blue flowers with a white base to the petals.

The bright red flowers of Geum quellyon *'Mrs. Bradshaw' are visible from across the garden.*

GEUM (JEE-um)
Avens

About 60 showy but short-lived species reside with this genus. Many are small enough for the rock garden, while one or two are sufficiently large enough to be included in the "mainstream" garden. The five-petaled flowers appear in the spring and may be red, yellow, orange, or white. In general, plants perform better and persist longer in the North than in the South. Propagate by seed or division after flowering is complete.

QUELLYON (QUELL-EE-on)
Chilean Avens
Colors: Red and scarlet
Zones: 5 to 7
○

The most common species available, Chilean avens (also known as *G. chiloense*) is most showy when sited correctly. Plants bear 1-inch-wide scarlet flowers over 6- to 12-inch-long lobed hairy leaves. Although plants are brilliant, they persist for only about two years. They look good in the spring, but in areas of hot summers, decline quite rapidly. The species has been superseded by a number of cultivars, most of which are seed propagated and easily available.

Cultivars

'Dolly North' has orange semidouble flowers.

'Fire Opal' bears intense red semidouble flowers.

'Lady Stratheden' is offered by many nurseries and produces buttercup yellow semidouble flowers.

'Mrs. Bradshaw' is the most popular cultivar, bearing scarlet semidouble flowers. In the cases of this and the preceding cultivar, they have their moments of glory but usually produce too many leaves for the number of flowers.

'Princess Juliana' bears soft yellow semidouble flowers that open a little later than most others.

The clear white flowers of creeping baby's breath, Gypsophila repens *'Fratensis', tumble over rocks with abandon.*

GYPSOPHILA (GYP-SOFF-ILL-A)
Baby's Breath

Who has received a bouquet of flowers without those ubiquitous thin stems of small white baby's breath flowers? If one thinks of the hundreds of thousands of cut flowers sold by florists, each one with a stem or two of baby's breath, the commercial importance of this plant quickly becomes evident. However, although some people still believe milk comes from stores, baby's breath need not come only from florists (and it takes much less room than a cow).

Plants of common baby's breath (*G. paniculata*) are relatively large, growing 3 feet tall and equally wide. They do particularly well on the West Coast and in the Midwest and are hardy from Zones 3 to 9. The plants need a well-drained sunny location and do better in soils with high amounts of calcium. Generally such areas have a neutral to basic pH (6.5 to 7.5), known in garden jargon as sweet soil. If you are successful growing rhododendrons, you likely will be unsuccessful growing baby's breath in the same area. Plants are all the more handsome for their gray-green leaves, and when in bloom in early summer, the flowers have a whimsical wispy appearance. A well-grown specimen is absolutely white with flowers, and the more they are picked, the more new flowers appear. Amend the area with dolomitic limestone and include a few plants. Add a few roses and you have your own mini-florist. Propagate by terminal cuttings.

Cultivars

'Bristol Fairy' grows 2 to 2½ feet tall and has double white flowers. Used extensively in the commercial business of cut-flower production.

'Nana' is more dwarf than other cultivars, yet the branches are long enough to still be used for cutting. Flowers are white.

'Perfecta' bears large white flowers and is a bit more robust than 'Bristol Fairy'.

'Pink Star' has pink flowers on an 18-inch-tall, compact frame.

'Red Sea' produces double rose-pink flowers on stems 3 to 4 feet tall.

Related Species

G. repens (creeping baby's breath) is a terrific ground-hugging plant for the front of the garden or the rock garden. It measures only 18 inches tall and is covered with white flowers in early summer.

'Pink Beauty' and 'Rosea' have handsome pink flowers and 'Fratensis' bears larger, creamy white flowers. The species is not as pH sensitive as its big brother and can be planted in any well-drained sunny site.

* HELENIUM (HEL-EE-NE-UM)
Sneezeweed

The majority of the 35 to 40 species in this genus are American natives but *H. autumnale* (common sneezeweed) is the easiest to locate. Sneezeweed is native to eastern North America and produces colorful daisies in late summer and fall. Although hardy from Zones 3 to 8, plants perform best in cool summers and become tall and lanky if grown in areas with warm night temperatures. The 2- to 3-inch-wide flowers occur in many colors and are borne on plants 3 to 5 feet tall. Plant in full sun, fertilize sparingly, and cut back after flowering. Propagate by division in the spring every two or three years.

Cultivars

Numerous cultivars are available, many of which are hybrids among *H. autumnale*, *H. bigelovii* (bigelow sneezeweed), and *H. hoopesii* (orange sneezeweed). For southern gardeners, the shorter forms should be chosen.

Flowers of Helenium autumnale *'Riverton Beauty' dominate in the fall garden.*

'Brilliant' produces hundreds of bronze flowers on plants 4 feet tall.

'Bruno' bears bronze-red flowers on stems 3 to 4 feet tall.

'Butterpat' is a popular cultivar with good reason. This plant grows 4 to 5 feet tall and yellow petals surround a bronze cylindrical center cone.

'Crimson Beauty', only 2 to 3 feet tall, bears orange flowers with brown centers. Flowers are produced earlier than on other cultivars.

'Gartensonne' is 6 feet tall with primrose yellow flowers and reddish brown centers.

'Riverton Beauty' produces golden yellow flowers around bronze centers on plants 3 to 4 feet tall.

'The Bishop' is likely a cultivar of *H. bigelovii* and has clean yellow flowers on plants 2 to 2½ feet tall. An excellent dwarf cultivar.

'Wyndley' bears coppery brown flowers on stems 2 to 3 feet tall. Plants are also early.

＊ *HELIANTHUS*
(HEE-LEE-AN-THUS)
Sunflower

The common sunflower has come a long way in recent years. While most people know sunflowers from Van Gogh's paintings or as food for their bird feeders, perennial sunflowers make magnificent garden plants in late summer and fall. The perennial types bear many more flowers, although smaller in size, and are also less prone to disease and pests than the annual forms.

Reaching heights of 4 to 5 feet, the flower-laden stems of Helianthus angustifolius *tower over other plants in the fall border.*

ANGUSTIFOLIUS
(AN-GUS-TI-FO-lee-us)
Swamp Sunflower
Color: Yellow
Zones: 6 to 9
○

One of the finest species for the fall garden, plants can provide a wonderful display or a weedy mess, depending on how they are handled. Many 2-inch-wide bright yellow flowers occur in mid-September through November on plants 4 to 7 feet tall. The deep green leaves are about 1 inch wide and are borne the entire length of the plant. Plants must be planted in full sun; partial shade results in tall (up to 10 feet), lanky plants that fall over in heavy rains and winds. In short, lack of sun equals sunflower weeds. If partial shade can't be avoided, pinch the plants in May or June. Plants are heavy feeders and require abundant water to perform their best. The only drawback is their propensity to multiply rapidly, producing little forests of sunflowers where there was once only one. Divide in the fall or spring, save one or two for yourself, and provide gifts to needier gardens with the others.

Related Species

All of the perennial sunflowers are large and bear many yellow daisy flowers in late summer and fall.

H. giganteus (giant sunflower) commonly grows 8 feet tall in the sun and even taller in partial shade. A terrific plant for large gardens, it is covered with 2- to 2½-inch-wide buttercup yellow flowers in the fall. This plant is more cold tolerant than *H. angustifolius*.

H. salicifolius (willow sunflower) bears very narrow (½- to ¾-inch-wide) leaves. The foliage is the most handsome of the group.

One of my favorites is a relatively unknown native of South Carolina, *H. schweinitzii* (Schweinitz sunflower). With approximately the same range of hardiness as the swamp sunflower, it is covered with small yellow flowers on 6-foot-tall plants. The difference is that Schweinitz sunflower doesn't scream through the garden like a banshee, an endearing characteristic for the many gardeners who love the sunflowers but get tired of removing unwanted offspring. I have grown this plant for four years and it has always been well behaved.

HELLEBORUS
(HELL-E-BOR-us)
Hellebore

The hellebores consist of nearly 20 species and go under such wonderful names as Christmas

The easiest of hellebores to grow, flowers of lenten rose, Helleborus orientalis, *appear in late winter and continue into late spring.*

rose, Lenten rose, and bear's-foot rose. Hellebores don't really look like roses, don't smell like roses, and don't even belong to the rose family. But, like the rose, to know them is to love them.

FOETIDUS (FOY-TI-DUS)
Bear's-Foot Rose, Bear's-Foot Hellebore
Color: Green
Zones: 5 to 9

Underused and underappreciated, the bear's-foot hellebore is a study in plant growth and morphology. The flower buds form in the fall and look as if they are almost ready to open by late December. They just keep swelling, regardless of the abysmal weather, and finally open in February in the South and April in the North. *H. foetidus* is wonderfully handsome with its light green nodding flowers and fingerlike dark green foliage. While not as handsome in flower as the Lenten or Easter rose (*H. niger* and *H. orientalis*), it is fascinating for a much longer time. Half the fun of gardening is the anticipation of flowering; with this species, you can watch the evolution from tiny buds to lovely flowers over a three- to four-month period. Plant in well-drained soils in partial shade. Provide an area with good ventilation, such as under pine or oak; refrain from placing plants close to a hedge or other air-blocking structure. If not properly sited, they suffer from a foliage disease (black spot), which results in blackening of the foliage and plant death within two years. Plants resent being disturbed. The best means of propagation is from self-sown seedlings at the base of the plant.

Cultivars

'Wester Flisk' is similar to the species with a more purplish tinge to the flowers.

ORIENTALIS (O-REE-EN-TAH-LIS)
Lenten Rose
Colors: White and purple
Zones: 4 to 9

If one can choose but one "rose," let it be this one. Plants form large colonies within three years, flower prolifically for months at a time, and are seldom attacked by pests or diseases. Not only are they the easiest of the hellebores to grow (much easier than the finicky Christmas rose, *H. niger*), the flowers can be used as long-lasting cut flowers. The dark green leaves are evergreen, although winter damage due to cold and wind can blacken some of the foliage; cut off the damaged portions in early spring, and new growth will soon take its place. Flowers are initiated in the fall but, unlike those of bear's-foot hellebore, don't appear until the spring. The white-to-purple flowers are formed in early spring (late winter in the South) and persist for at least eight weeks.

Although seed can be purchased, it is notoriously slow to germinate. The best bet is to transplant the self-sown seedlings found at the base of the plants to small pots for growing on. Put in the garden when large enough to be transplanted.

Cultivars

Cultivars are seldom available in the United States because of the length of time required to propagate them. More than 80 named cultivars and hybrids have been selected in Europe, and it is curious that so few are available here. However, aggressive breeding and selection programs are underway in this country and, without doubt, some will soon be offered.

VENUSTA (VEN-EWS-TA)
Dwarf Hosta
Color: Lilac
Zones: 3 to 9

While dwarf species cannot compete in stature and overall effect with larger hybrids, I include *H. venusta* for its beauty and usefulness in small shaded areas. I have a few plants tucked among rocks around my garden pond, and although I must be nearly on top of them to appreciate them, I cannot think of any better choice for those sites. Plants are 3 to 4 inches tall, about 8 inches wide and spread well. The green foliage is handsome but the variegated forms are far more appealing.

Cultivars

'Variegata' has creamy white centers surrounded by green margins. Definitely an improvement on the species. Plants are slower growing than the species, so if room permits, plant at least three in a given area.

Love them or hate them, the multicolored leaves of Houttuynia cordata *'Chameleon' always elicit strong responses from gardeners.*

HOUTTUYNIA (HOO-TIE-NEE-A)
Chameleon Plant

Here is a plant for everyone, including people who love plants as well as those who love to make fun of people who love plants. It is known as *H. cordata*, with heart-shaped green leaves and small white flowers. The variegated forms are the most handsome and useful. Plants are terrific in many ways. They can be grown almost anywhere, from full sun in "normal" soil to partially shaded water gardens. In fact, chameleon plant is an aquatic plant and at home in boggy areas. The foliage can be extremely colorful, with bright splotches of purple, pink, and red. In the cooler times of the season, the leaves look like an elf has spilled paint all over them. However, one should be careful about embracing this plant too quickly—there is a catch or two. One should not, in fact, embrace this plant at all. Although I have seen references to the lemony fragrance of the foliage, I use this plant to demonstrate to my students just how bad plants can smell. After tearing off a leaf and taking a whiff, they make a face and say something unprintable about my teaching methods. Another catch is that, once introduced to the garden, chameleon plant generally wants to take over. It reminds me of mint in the way in which it invades, defying eradication and reveling in its obnoxious behavior. Lastly, the beauty of the variegated foliage often reverts to the plain green of the species. I can occasionally handle smelly, invasive plants if they provide sufficient beauty, but in my garden this plant is history when it reneges on its promise of colorful foliage. Gardeners in the South find more reversion than those in the North, likely the result of warmer temperatures. To each his own.

Cultivars

'Chameleon' ('Variegata') has multicolored leaves and ½-inch-long white flowers with slightly raised centers. It is the most common cultivar.

'Flore-plena' has green leaves tinged with purple and double white flowers.

HYPERICUM (HY-PER-I-CUM)
St.-John's-Wort

Numerous species of St.-John's-wort are grown in gardens throughout the country but only about half a dozen are commonly available. The bright yellow shining flowers have five petals, five sepals, and hundreds of stamens that give the flower its other wonderful name, Aaron's-beard. Some of the species are useful groundcovers (*H. calycinum, H. olympicum, H. polyphyllum*), while others are shrubby and may stand up to 3 feet high (*H. patulum*). The leaves are generally opposite or whorled and dark green.

CALYCINUM (KAL-I-SIGH-NUM)
Aaron's-Beard
Color: Yellow
Zones: 5 to 8

Probably the best of the groundcover forms, Aaron's-beard can blanket large areas with plants 15 to 18 inches tall. In the spring, the roselike, 2- to 3-inch-wide flowers brighten up the area and flowers persist for about six weeks. While the flowers are showy and colorful, the strength of the plant lies in the classic, season-long beauty of the foliage. The dull blue-green foliage is so perfect and soothing that one wants to lie down in the planting for a pleasant night's sleep. Summer hardy to Zone 8, plants perform equally well in the South and North. If temperatures are too warm, flowers are borne poorly or not at all. In areas of cold blustery winters, desiccating winds and cold, dry air result in brown or fallen leaves, which turn brown around the edges. Propagate plants by division, or by terminal cuttings after flowering has finished.

OLYMPICUM (O-LIM-PI-KUM)
Olympic St.-John's-Wort
Color: Yellow
Zones: 6 to 8

This small St.-John's-wort measures only about a foot in height and is equally wide. The gray-green foliage is attached to trailing stems and plants are particularly handsome tucked in around rocks or at the front of the border. The

Covering the ground with clean green foliage and marvelous yellow flowers, Hypericum calycinum *crawls throughout Butchard Gardens in Victoria, British Columbia.*

flowers may be up to 2 inches wide and are relatively large compared to the stature of the plant. Plants tolerate warm temperatures; they have performed well in Athens, Georgia, and are remarkable in Long Island, New York; Denver, Colorado; and Seattle, Washington. Propagate as for *H. calycinum*.

Cultivars

Var. *citrinum* bears absolutely lovely pale yellow flowers. It is the most handsome form of the species.

Var. *minus* is a little smaller than the species. This form is often listed as *H. polyphyllum*. The leaves are slightly grayer and plants should be used more often. 'Sulphureum' has fine sulfur-yellow flowers.

Looking like a snowbank in spring, the flowers of Iberis sempervirens *'Snowflake' always seem fresh.*

IBERIS (EYE-BEER-IS)
Candytuft

One of the toughest and easiest perennials to grow, candytuft has been around forever and will continue to be a mainstay for years to come. Although approximately 40 species are known, the most successful is *I. sempervirens* (candytuft) and may be obtained from almost every nursery and retail center. The 9- to 12-inch-tall plants are best used in the front of the garden or as edging and perform well in sunny locations in well-drained soils. The small 1-inch-long leaves remain evergreen (although they are nothing to write home about during the winter). The flowers, which persist for up to 10 weeks, are held in a 1- to 2-inch-wide inflorescence and are invariably white or cream colored. Plants are woody at the base and should be cut back hard every two years to reduce legginess. Propagate the species from seed. Most cultivars are raised from terminal cuttings.

Cultivars

There is little difference among many cultivars. All flowers are in shades of white (clean or dirty), and plants differ in their degree of dwarfness.

'Autumn Snow' is 8 to 10 inches tall and has large, clear white flowers. It blooms in the spring and again in the fall.

'Little Gem' is only 5 to 8 inches tall with small clear white flowers.

'Purity' has lustrous, green leaves and an abundance of flowers on 8- to 10-inch plants.

'Nana' ('Pygmaea') almost hugs the ground and shoots up small white flowers in the spring.

'Snowflake' is a marvelous plant 8 to 10 inches tall with 2- to 3-inch-wide inflorescences. One of the most popular candytufts.

INULA (IN-YEW-LA)
Inula

Some wonderful species of *Inula* occur and generally are large coarse plants with yellow flowers. While approximately 60 species have been described, only 2 or 3 are commonly available.

One of the smaller members of the genus, Inula ensifolia *looks best at the front of the garden.*

ENSIFOLIA (EN-SI-FO-LEE-A)
Swordleaf Inula
Color: Yellow
Zones: 3 to 7
○

One of the smallest species in the genus, plant produces numerous yellow-to-orange daisylike flowers. Mature specimens are only 2 feet tall. Although tolerant of heat and humidity as far south as north Georgia, plants are more vigorous in Zones 4 to 6. Plants are generally short-lived and should not be expected to persist more than four years. They prefer well-drained soils. Propagate by terminal cuttings or seed.

Cultivars

'Compacta' is more compact than the species.

MAGNIFICA (MAG-NI-FI-CA)
Large Inula
Color: Yellow
Zones: 3 to 7
○

This 6- to 7-foot-tall plant is most impressive in a sunny, moist site and bears many flowers 3 to 4 inches in diameter. In areas of hot summers, plants may require support; in cool summers, plants are more compact and stronger. If one has a place for a large, somewhat coarse plant and can provide consistent moisture, try this bold specimen.

The yellow waxy flowers of Kirengoshoma palmata are short lived but beautiful.

Bold flowers rise like bicolored trees over the grassy foliage of Kniphofia 'Atlanta'

KIRENGESHOMA
(KI-RENG-GE-SHOW-MA)
Yellow Waxbells
Zones: 5 to 7

A most handsome plant when properly sited; the lovely light green palmate leaves grow into significant clumps. Waxbells are so named because of the waxy yellow bell-shaped flowers that hang in clusters from the upper left axils in late summer and fall. Unfortunately, flowers begin to turn brown in a few days, a problem made worse if plants are not consistently moist. The flowers give way to ghoulish horned fruit, interesting if not particularly ornamental. When growing well, plants are worth having in the garden; however, they must be placed in semishade, sheltered from strong winds, provided with an abundant source of organic matter, and kept consistently moist. If such a site is available, they are worth a try. Allow plants to remain undisturbed. If propagation is necessary, divisions may be taken in the spring after three to five years.

KNIPHOFIA (NEE-FOF-EE-A)
Red-hot Poker, Torch Lily
Zones: 5 to 8

Most of the plants offered in the United States are cultivars or hybrids of common torch lily, *K. uvaria.* The coarse gray-green evergreen foliage provides contrast to fine-leaved plants in the garden, and the colorful flowers of many cultivars can be seen "for miles." Plants thrive in Zones 5 to 8 and require full sun for best performance. Many individual flowers form a colorful spike 4 to 5 feet tall and, although eye-catching, they generally persist for less than two weeks. In the species itself, while the uppermost flowers on the spike are bright red or scarlet, the bottom ones have already finished and are yellowish green. This nonuniformity of flowering results in a two-tone flower spike. The flowers of many of the newer cultivars open more uniformly on the spike for a result that is less bicolored. Plants are relatively drought tolerant and return year after year. If the long pointed leaves are messy after flowering, simply cut them halfway back; this may be done without injury to the plant. Propagate by seed or division after flowering.

Cultivars

All cultivars are essentially hybrids. Most flower in late spring to early summer, but late bloomers may not flower until fall.

'Atlanta' is 2 to 3 feet tall and bears bright orange-scarlet flowers with a pale yellow base. A great plant for a great city.

'Glow' produces coral-red flowers and stands about 2½ feet tall.

'Little Maid' has narrow foliage and attractive creamy white flowers. The plant is only 18 to 24 inches tall.

'Maid of Orleans' has ivory flowers on stems 2 to 2½ feet tall. Flowers are much more soothing than those of the species.

'Primrose Beauty' bears primrose yellow flowers on stems 3 feet tall.

'Sunningdale Yellow' is one of the finest yellow-flowered torch lilies I have ever laid eyes on. Only 2 to 3 feet tall, it draws people like a magnet from everywhere in the garden.

'Wayside Flame' bears late-flowering, deep orange-red, 3-foot-tall flower spikes.

LAMIUM (LAY-MEE-UM)
Dead Nettle

Plants in the genus provide useful 8- to 12-inch-tall groundcovers for semishaded locations. The main species available to the American gardener is *L. maculatum* (spotted nettle). The 1- to 2-inch-long leaves are generally variegated or bear white stripes on the upper surfaces. If grown in Zones 3 to 6, plants are rapid growers and fill in quickly. Although they are reasonably effective

The rosy red flowers of Lamium maculatum *cover the foliage when properly sited.*

in Zones 7 and 8, they tend to melt out in the summer heat even if adequate shade is provided. The red-to-purple flowers associated with the species can be spectacular and take a back seat to the foliage. Propagate by division anytime or by terminal cuttings in the spring. In southern gardens, plants should be rejuvenated and replaced every three years.

Cultivars

'Beacon Silver' has silver leaves bordered by green margins. The foliage stands out well even in shady areas. An excellent, heat-tolerant cultivar that grows 6 to 8 inches tall.

'Chequers' has silver variegated leaves and amethyst-violet flowers. It is 9 to 12 inches tall.

'White Nancy' is similar to 'Beacon Silver' but has white flowers. Plants require shade; full sun must be avoided. This has become the cultivar of choice in many American gardens.

LIATRIS (LIE-A-TRIS)
Gayfeather, Blazing Star

Numerous species of blazing star occur, all indigenous to North America. It is one of the treasures of American flora and it is satisfying to see more nurseries carrying a range of native species for the American gardener. All bear spires of purple-to-white flowers that open from the top down, a rather unusual occurrence in spikelike stems. Most species do well in dry soils; rich soils generally result in lanky growth and poor-quality plants. The most satisfying species for most gardeners is the 2- to 4-foot *L. spicata* (spike gayfeather) and is available in shades of lavender and white. Plants must be provided with a sunny location, for if planted in too much shade, flowers seldom appear or are of poor quality. Flowers make excellent cut stems and should be cut when about two-thirds of the spike is open. Plants may be divided by lifting and dividing the knobby roots in the fall.

The lavender-purple flowers of Liatris spicata 'Kobold' appear in late spring and summer in the sunny garden.

Cultivars

'August Glory' bears purple flowers on stems 3 to 4 feet tall.

'Floristan White' is about 3 feet tall and bears creamy white flowers.

'Kobold' is probably the best cultivar for most gardeners. Two and a half feet tall, it bears numerous spikes of lilac-mauve flowers in early summer. This plant is stout and self-supporting.

LIGULARIA
(LIG-YEW-LAYER-EE-A)
Ligularia

Some outstanding species and cultivars may be found under this genus, but site selection is all-important in the performance of these plants. If the site receives steady rainfall or is somewhat boggy, then the bold foliage and flowers of ligu-

laria live up to expectations. They also are more satisfying in areas of cool night temperatures, such as the Northeast or Northwest, and are frustrating where night temperatures remain above 70 degrees Fahrenheit. Warm night temperatures and dry soils are anathema to all members of the genus. However, few plants make such a bold statement if well grown and they are worth trying at least once.

DENTATA (DEN-TAH-TA)
Big-leaf Ligularia
Color: Yellow
Zones: 4 to 7

Grown mainly for foliage effect, the large, dark-purple-to-green kidney-shaped leaves may be up to 20 inches wide. Large clumps are particularly impressive and form lovely backdrops for other more colorful species. The 3- to 4-foot-tall and equally wide plants bear deep yellow daisy flowers that look like they are wilting even when first open. Spectacular when well sited and gruesome when not, big-leaf ligularia is surely not for everyone. Like most other plants, it looks good almost anywhere in the spring. One should not be fooled into embracing this species until one falls in love with it in the summer. Plants may be multiplied by division in the spring or seed.

Cultivars

'Desdemona' has deep purple foliage with dark green tops and purple bases even in hot weather—one of the most heat-tolerant cultivars. Leaves are beet red upon emergence.

'Othello' is similar but a bit more compact.

In moist, partially shaded areas, the flowers of Ligularia stenocephala *'The Rocket' explode in early summer.*

'Gregynog Gold' is a hybrid with bright orange flowers held on an upright conical inflorescence over richly veined heart-shaped leaves. It grows 4 to 6 feet tall.

'Sungold' bears flowers held well above the foliage and shown off much better than on other cultivars.

STENOCEPHALA
(STEN-O-SEF-A-LA)
Narrow-spiked Ligularia
Color: Yellow
Zones: 4 to 7

While *L. dentata* is best grown for its foliage, this one is well known for the 12- to 18-inch-long spikelike yellow flowers. The light green leaves are triangular to heart shaped and lose large amounts of water. The 4- to 5-foot-tall flower spikes are most impressive and useful design components.

Cultivars

'The Rocket' is widely available and represents the species in many gardens. This compact plant bears 18- to 24-inch-long stems of smaller lemon yellow flowers and looks particularly good with other spiky flowers such as *Cimicifuga*.

LINUM (LY-NUM)
Flax

Grown for many years for oil and fiber, flax is a lovely ornamental plant as well. Beautiful seas of blue flax still wave in the summer breeze in many fields of Europe. Linseed oil is derived from the seeds of the annual flax, *L. usitatissimum*. Numerous species have been described but only three or four are used in American gardens. The perennial species usually found in nurseries

White, rather than blue flowers, cover the plants of Linum perenne *'Album'.*

is perennial flax, *L. perenne*. The wiry 12-inch-tall stems bear small narrow leaves, and the light blue ¾-inch-wide flowers are produced from late spring through summer. Flowering is persistent under good conditions and flowers stay open for longer than 12 weeks. Flax performs well in full sun and well-drained soils, but abhors wet feet. Plants are hardy from Zones 4 to 8, but as summers get hotter, the need for good drainage becomes more critical. If plants get leggy in the heat, cut back to 8 to 10 inches after flowering.

Cultivars

'Album' consists of 12- to 15-inch-tall plants bearing creamy white flowers on upright stems. Plants are widely available.

'Saphir' ('Saphyr') bears deep blue flowers and is more compact (8 to 12 inches) than the species. An excellent garden form.

Liriope spicata is thought of as a tough groundcover, but the flowers also provide a marvelous display in the summer.

LIRIOPE (LEAR-REE-OPE) or (LEA-RYE-O-PEE)
Lily-Turf
Zones: 6 to 10

One cannot travel in the southern half of the United States and not see drifts of lily-turf in private gardens and public arenas. The main species is *L. muscari* (common lily-turf) and it is particularly useful as edging and groundcover in difficult growing areas. Some people feel that *Liriope* is overused, and while some lazy designers and gardeners are not creative enough to find alternatives, it is nevertheless an excellent, tough plant, handsome in leaf, flower and fruit. Place in full sun, although partial shade is tolerated, and cut back in the early spring to about 6 inches. I use a lawn mower for my pruning needs. The straplike foliage contrasts with the spiky lilac flowers that give way to black berries in the fall. Space plants 8 to 12 inches apart, fertilize in the spring, and allow them to run through the area and create a dark green carpet. If plants become overcrowded or if additional plants are needed, divide anytime to your heart's content. The roots are tough, so be sure you limber up before going on the attack.

Cultivars

'Gold-banded' has wide arching leaves with a narrow gold band down the middle, and lavender flowers.

'Lilac Beauty' has stiff lilac flower clusters held well above the green foliage.

'Majestic' has deep lilac flowers with green foliage.

'Munroe White' bears white flowers over green leaves.

seen is one in which the plants were placed in a narrow rectangular bed surrounded on one side by a driveway and on the other by a garage. Hardly romantic, but effective. If its roaming habit is not a nuisance, plants are well worth growing. The flowers are excellent as cut flowers, and with a simple floral preservative purchased at any garden shop, flowers persist well over a week. Propagate by division in the spring or seed.

Related Species

L. ephemerum (silvery loosestrife) has silver-green foliage but bears flowers similar to those of gooseneck loosestrife. It is much less invasive and highly desirable.

NUMMULARIA
(NUM-EW-LAH-REE-A)
Creeping Jenny
Color: Yellow
Zones: 3 to 7

Native to Europe, this groundcover has become naturalized in much of the eastern United States. The bright yellow flowers are borne in the axils of the opposite leaves. The plants grow to only about 8 inches in height and spread by long stems that root at the leaf nodes. They prefer partial shade and moist areas; if too dry, they struggle. The most popular cultivar is 'Aurea', known as golden creeping Jenny or just plain golden Jenny. The foliage is lime green to almost yellow and is guaranteed to brighten up shady areas in the garden. Similar to other species of Lysimachia, its creeping tendencies can become overbearing. Many gardeners have been known to get their exercise by playing tug of war with the stems of creeping Jenny. Unfortunately, Jenny usually wins. Propagate by divisions in spring or fall.

A large clump of Macleaya cordata dwarfs the yellow flowers of Rudbeckia fulgida var. deamii.

MACLEAYA (MACK-LAY-YA)
Plume Poppy
Zones: 3 to 8

"One man's ceiling is another man's floor" expresses the relationship between the plume poppy (M. cordata) and gardeners throughout the world. These 6- to 10-foot-tall plants are known for their large, hairy, heart-shaped leaves and the impressive creamy plume flowers on top. As a specimen plant in full sun or partial shade, used to block unpleasant vistas or simply to draw the eye to its part of the garden, plume poppy is hard to beat. It is large and requires sufficient room to spread—and spread it does. Plantlets are produced by running root stalks, and soon dozens of little "maclets" are hovering around their mother. If the area is large enough for such a gathering, this is a wonderful plant. People who wish to enjoy the beauty but not the rowdiness can place plume poppy in large decorative containers. The upright growth accentuates the plant's beauty, but the container enforces discipline. Use the containers as accents by the driveway or even to show off the entrance by the front door. Propagate by digging the maclets and placing them elsewhere.

The blue flowers of Mertensia virginica *are an indispensible part of the spring garden.*

* *MERTENSIA* (MER-TEN-SEE-A)
Bluebells
Zones: 3 to 8

Without Virginia bluebells, spring is not complete. Numerous species of bluebells occur, but only one is commonly offered, our native Virginia bluebell (*M. virginica*). Although other species are handsome, few can compete with the emphemeral beauty of this species. Plants emerge in early spring, and before long, clusters of 5 to 20 flowers appear in the nodes of the smooth, light green leaves. Virginia bluebells are native to Virginia and much of the eastern seaboard. Full sun is tolerated in northern climes but partial shade and moist soil are best in the South. The only drawback to the inclusion of plants in the garden is that they go dormant by midsummer. Plant with annuals or late-emerging perennials like balloonflower (*Platycodon grandiflorus*) to cover up the area left vacant. Propagate by fresh seed or division in the spring. Other species, such as Siberian bluebells (*M. sibirica*) and Italian bluebells (*M. italica*), have great potential as garden plants if they can be located.

Plants of Monarda didyma *'Cambridge Scarlet' produce an abundance of flowers in early summer.*

MONARDA (MO-NARD-A)
Bee Balm
Zones: 4 to 8

A mainstay in many gardens, bee balm provides some lovely moments as well as anxious ones. Although about a dozen species are known, *M. didyma*, the 2- to 4-foot-tall common bee-balm, or Oswego tea, is easiest to locate and grow. Hardy from Zones 4 to 8, bee balm should be provided with moist soils and a sunny to partially shaded site. Partial shade is best if soils tend to dry out. The stem is noticeably four-sided and the flowers in the species are red. To see the brilliant flowers of *Monarda* glowing from stream banks along the Blue Ridge Parkway in North Carolina is spectacular. Nowhere in this stand of bee balm could I find any powdery mildew, the bane of this plant in the cultivated garden. The combination of too much sun and too little moisture in the garden likely causes plant stress, resulting in mildew. Plants tend to reproduce from underground stems and significant populations can appear. A good plant for the North, poor at best in the South. Numerous cultivars have been produced, some of which are hybrids with *M. fistulosa* (wild bergamot).

Cultivars

'Adam' bears cerise flowers and is more compact (2 to 2½ feet), an excellent improvement.

'Cambridge Scarlet' (2 to 3 feet) produces flaming scarlet flowers on vigorous plants.

'Croftway Pink' is similar to 'Cambridge Scarlet' and has soft pink flowers.

'Mahogany' has dark red flowers, close to black, and is 2 to 4 feet tall.

'Panorama' bears plants of many colors on stems 3 feet tall. Propagate from seed.

'Snow Maiden' provides creamy white flowers on stems 3 feet tall and combines well with other summer flowers.

* *OENOTHERA* (EE-NO-THE-RA)
Evening Primrose, Sundrop

More than 150 species of evening primrose are native to the United States and range in color from yellow and pink to white. Some species bear flowers that open in the evening (known as evening primroses), and others open during the day (sundrops). All species perform best in full sun. Some are particularly invasive.

Handsome flowers are produced for weeks on vigorous plants of Oenothera speciosa 'Rosea'.

MISSOURIENSIS
(MI-SUR-REN-SIS)
Ozark Sundrops
Color: Yellow
Zones: 4 to 8
◯

Bearing some of the largest flowers in the genus, Ozark sundrops produce solitary paper-thin bright yellow flowers up to 4 inches across. The sepals are often spotted red in the bud stage and the red hue remains even when open. Plants are only 6 to 12 inches tall but make an enormous splash when in bloom. They struggle a little in the summer heat in the South, but some cultivars are more heat tolerant than others. Flowering occurs in late spring and summer, and plants persist for three to five years.

Cultivars

'Greencourt Lemon' is a marvelous cultivar with sulphur yellow 4-inch-wide flowers. Heat tolerant and persistent, it is an excellent cultivar.

SPECIOSA (SPEE-SEE-O-SA)
Showy Evening Primrose
Color: Rose-pink
Zones: 4 to 9
◯

A plant that reminds me of a con artist who is so good at his work that you can't help but respect his skill, no matter how misdirected. A seemingly innocent-looking plantlet, no bigger than a tomato transplant, can romp through the garden in a single season leaving a trail of offspring in its wake. However, no matter how one grumbles as plantlets are discarded in the fall, one cannot argue with the effectiveness of the many rose-pink flowers. Starting in early spring,

flowers 1 to 2 inches in diameter smother the dark green foliage and continue well into the summer. There is no doubt that the species should be considered invasive with a capital "I," but what a show it provides. In our garden we now have our plants in a small island bed surrounded by sidewalk and a building. The island is already crowded. Plants are only 12 to 18 inches tall and are easily divided anytime. 'Rosea' is sometimes offered with flowers that appear to be a little larger and deeper in color than the species.

TETRAGONA (TET-RA-GO-NA)
Four-angled Sundrop
Color: Yellow
Zones: 3 to 7
◯

Bushy and bright, well-grown plants produce many 1- to 1½-inch-wide bright yellow flowers on plants 1 to 3 feet tall in late spring and summer. Although native to eastern North America, they are not as heat tolerant as other species of sundrops and are best treated as biennials or short-lived perennials in southern gardens. The species is seldom grown, but some excellent cultivars have been selected.

Cultivars

'Fireworks' ('Fyrverkeri') is about 18 inches tall with red stems. Buds with bright yellow flowers 1½ to 2 inches wide appear in late spring and summer. More compact than the species, it may be placed near the front or middle of the garden.

'Highlights' ('Hohes Licht') grows only about 1 foot tall and bears 1½-inch-wide yellow flowers.

Solstice' ('Sonnenwende') bears many red flower buds that open into a shower of clear yellow flowers. Plants are about 2 feet tall.

'Yellow River' has larger flowers (2 inches wide) and stands up to 2½ feet tall.

Other Species

O. perennis, nodding sundrops, is heat tolerant and persistent in southern gardens. Plants are 1 to 2 feet tall with dozens of large yellow flowers that burst open from red buds in late spring.

Clean white flowers of Ornithogalum umbellatum *appear throughout the spring garden like clockwork every year.*

ORNITHOGALUM
(OR-NITH-OG-A-LUM)
Ornithogalum

This genus consists of about 100 species of bulb plants, most of which come from Europe. A number have been grown commercially as cut flowers for many years while others have become established garden plants. Gardeners in the Northwest and Northeast enjoy far more success with *Ornithogalum* than others. *O. umbellatum*, however, has colonized gardens everywhere.

UMBELLATUM
(UM-BEL-AYE-TUM)
Star-of-Bethlehem
Color: White
Zones: 4 to 8

A handsome flower borne over a mound of straplike foliage and ease of growing have made this a favorite in gardens throughout the country. It is one of the cleanest whites of white-flowered plants I have observed. While some people may think it a weed, Leonardo da Vinci surely did not when he painted it in 1620 in one of his finest renderings (now hanging in the Queen's collection in Windsor, England). Few requirements, other than a few hours of sun a day, are necessary for optimum performance. Approximately 10 star-shaped white flowers with green stripes are borne in the spring and persist for four to six weeks. Plants are 6 to 9 inches tall and the foliage essentially disappears by midsummer. They multiply well but are not obnoxious. Plants are easily multiplied by digging, separating smaller bulblets, and relocating elsewhere.

Patterns of shadows play over a handsome planting of Pachysandra terminalis *in Winterthur Garden in Delaware.*

PACHYSANDRA
(PA-KIS-AN-DRA)
Spurge

Pachysandra contains a number of excellent groundcovers. The most common, Japanese spurge (*P. terminalis*), has become a mainstay in public and private gardens throughout America. All species are tolerant of partial to heavy shade and are often found covering difficult areas under trees or in the constant shade of buildings.

*PROCUMBENS
(PRO-KUM-BENZ)
Allegheny Spurge
Color: White
Zones: 5 to 8

Seen far too little, this American native is more handsome, more persistent, and less prone to disease than common spurge (*P. terminalis*), yet is seldom offered by perennial nurseries. The main drawback is its relative slowness to fill in. Like the hare and the tortoise, the 9- to 12-inch-tall Allegheny spurge is just getting off the marks while its Japanese counterpart is hitting the homestretch. Nevertheless, its classic beauty seldom fails to impress, and in areas of partial shade and moist soils, Allegheny spurge is highly recommended.

TERMINALIS (TER-MI-NAH-LIS)
Japanese Spurge
Color: White
Zones: 4 to 8

Plants multiply by rhizomatous roots and carpet many gardens everywhere in the United States. The dark evergreen leaves are whorled near the tops of the stems and creamy white flowers are borne over them. A number of diseases, ranging from root rots to canker, are becoming more serious as more spurge is planted. Thinning and grooming of the colony is important in reducing the incidence of disease. While overused, a carpet of shining Japanese spurge protected by the high limbs of oak or chestnut is a magnificent sight.

'Twilight', also seed-propagated, produces 2-to 3-inch-long flowers in a mixture of colors.

DIGITALIS (DIG-I-TAH-LIS)

Color: White
Zones: 5 to 8

With heavily scented foliage and light blue flowers, Perovskia atriplicifolia *is a successful species in all sunny gardens.*

Relatively unknown in its native land, this native American species has been enjoyed by European gardeners for years. Plants grow 2 to 2½ feet tall and have smooth dark green leaves, over which are found large white tubular flowers. Plants are native from Maine to South Dakota and as far south as Texas. Although not as showy as the hybrids, they're more tolerant of temperature extremes. Flowers appear in early May in my garden and about a month later in northern states.

Cultivars

'Husker Red', an introduction fron the University of Nebraska, has excellent maroon-red foliage and white flowers. A wonderful plant with great design potential.

SMALLII (SMALL-EE-EYE)
Small's Penstemon

Color: Pinkish purple
Zones: 5 to 8

One of the most satisfying wild flowers I have grown, this species tolerates all sorts of temperature extremes, poor soils, and partial shade. Native to North Carolina and Tennessee, they bear tubular flowers with white on the insides. Although I have seen this species listed as growing to 4 feet in height, most are less than 2 feet tall. A must for penstemon lovers who have problems making the more showy forms look like their catalog pictures.

PEROVSKIA (PE-ROV-SKEE-A)
Russian Sage

Although several species occur, only *P. atriplicifolia* (common Russian sage) is offered to any extent in the United States. In spite of the less-than-overwhelming flower size and the odor of foot soldiers' boots when the leaves are crushed, the species is a favorite with gardeners everywhere.

ATRIPLICIFOLIA
(A-TRI-PLIS-I-FO-LEE-A)
Common Russian Sage
Color: Light blue
Zones: 3 to 8

This is the epitome of a plant to grow almost anywhere. Not only does it shine in my southeastern garden but it requires very little water and is a recommended xerophytic plant in Denver, Colorado, where rainfall is about 12 inches per year. Tolerant of heat, the species is also used with great success in North Dakota gardens. The small gray-green leaves provide a look of airiness. Small light blue tubular flowers are borne in whorls around the stems in mid- to late summer. Easy to grow, handsome in combination with any white-flowered plant, and resilient to abuse, this is a great beginner's plant. In the South, plants may be cut back in June to make them bushier and less sprawling. Provide adequate drainage; puddles around the root system are probably the only abuse to which it will succumb.

PERSICARIA (PER-SI-CAREE-A)
(syn. *Polygonum*)
Smartweed, Knotweed

This group of plants, commonly known as Polygonum, has been much defiled by a few aggres-

With its many rosy candles, Persicaria bistorta 'Superba' provides brilliant color in the early summer garden.

sive weeds (quite a few, really), and most people who have heard of the genus don't want to hear any more. The bad guys include Pennsylvania smartweed (*P. pensylvanicum*), common knotweed (*P. aviculare*), and lady's thumb (*P. persicaria*), all related and all painful to a gardener's psyche and back. However, if one keeps an open mind, the delights of a few other members are there to be discovered. In some cases, the aggressive behavior can be used to advantage (as in *P. cuspidatum*) or some can be refined garden plants (*P. bistorta*).

BISTORTA (BIS-TOR-TA)
Bistort, Snakeweed
Color: Pink
Zones: 3 to 7

This clump-forming species is handsome in foliage, bearing 5-inch-long wavy green leaves with striking white midribs. The soft pink flowers are held in upright spikes well above the foliage. The

stamens of the individual flowers protrude, giving spikes the appearance of bottle brushes. Place in well-drained soils. Unfortunately, plants do not perform well in warm climates. Most polygonums are limited to areas north of Zone 7.

Cultivars

'Superba' is the most common cultivar, and with larger plants and bigger flowers, it is superior to the species. Nice examples are found at Wave Hill, New York, and the Chicago Botanical Garden.

CUSPIDATA (KUS-PI-DAH-TA)
Mexican Bamboo
Color: Creamy white
Zones: 3 to 7
○

It is time to put aside prejudices concerning such tall colonizers as Mexican bamboo. These include mountain fleeceflower (*P. amplexicaulis*), *P. rude, P. sachalinense*, sacaline, and others. There is little doubt that they are not plants for the small garden, nor are they for the perennial border. Their aggressive behavior is legend and many pickaxes, shovels, and curses have been employed to rid gardens of unwanted plants. However, if used properly, they are noble, functional garden specimens. They are best as screens, hedging, or specimens in sunny, moist areas. Feathery inflorescences consisting of creamy white flowers are formed on the end of the hollow outward-curving stems. The red-brown stems are handsome in winter and may remain in the landscape until growth recurs in the spring. 'Crimson Beauty' bears wonderful blood-red flowers and is highly recommended. There is also a 2- to 3-foot-tall dwarf form, var. *compactum*, which, although better behaved, is far less graceful.

A *showy planting of* Phlox maculata *'Alpha' used by Post Property Management in Atlanta, GA, has proven tough as well as handsome.*

PHLOX (FLOKS)
Phlox

So many phlox, so little time! The number of garden-worthy species is amazing, ranging from groundcover forms such as moss phlox (*P. subulata*), midsize species like spotted phlox (*P. maculata*) to tall specimens such as garden phlox (*P. paniculata*). Within a plantsman's garden, likely another three or four species and countless cultivars would be encountered. All species are native to North America and thrive in diverse climates from Maine to Florida.

DIVARICATA (DI-VAH-RI-KAH-TA)
Woodland Phlox
Color: Lavender-blue
Zones: 3 to 8

Woodland phlox is one of those plants so easy for gardeners that it is ignored in favor of something new. Native to eastern North America, it may be grown over a wide range of temperatures. Plants are generally 12 to 15 inches tall, although some of the cultivars may be a good deal more prostrate. The petals of the blue flowers are slightly notched and the foliage consists of clean dark green oblong leaves. Place in partial shade, for as the common name suggests, they are woodland lovers. Consistent moisture is necessary for best performance.

Cultivars

'Dirigo Ice' ('Dirgo Ice') bears pale blue flowers on plants 8 to 12 inches tall.

'Fuller's White' is more dwarf (8 to 12 inches tall) and is completely covered with clean white notched flowers in the spring. If placed in partial shade and not allowed to dry out, plants resemble mounds of snow in April and May.

'Lamphamii', native to the western United States, produces dark blue flowers and entire (not notched) petals.

'Louisiana' is about 6 inches tall and bears early purple-blue flowers.

*MACULATA (MAK-EW-lah-ta)
Spotted Phlox
Colors: Various
Zones: 3 to 8
○

A fairly recent newcomer to the American commercial world, spotted phlox has found many converts. Called spotted phlox for the dark blotches on the stem, it grows 2 to 3 feet tall and bears dark green leaves arranged like steps on a ladder. The reason for its ascension from obscurity was some excellent breeding work (done in

Germany) that resulted in better colors and more compact growth. Most important of all, however, is its relative resistance to powdery mildew, a fungal disease that affects many cultivars of garden phlox (*P. paniculata*). Place in full sun and maintain good drainage. Although less mildew susceptible, if plants are stressed by difficult growing conditions, mildew can be a problem.

Cultivars

'Alpha' produces rosy pink flowers with a darker eye.

'Miss Lingard' early on produces white flowers with small yellow centers. While some of the newer cultivars outperform her, she brought the species out of obscurity and is still an excellent plant.

'Omega' bears white flowers with a small lilac eye and is a little more floriferous than 'Miss Lingard'.

'Rosalinde' has dark pink flowers.

*PANICULATA (PA-NIK-EW-LAH-TA)
Garden Phlox
Colors: Various
Zones: 3 to 7
○

By far the most common phlox on the market and arguably the most handsome. Many colors have been produced and some stunning cultivars exist. Up to 50 flowers may be borne on large inflorescences called panicles (thus its species name). The dark green leaves are opposite and if sited correctly are also ornamental. Powdery mildew has been a problem on some cultivars, and unfortunately many gardeners have given up on garden phlox because of this disfiguring problem. Provide good air circulation, sufficient drainage, and select cultivars with more mildew resistance than others. New cultivars are being selected for resistance and good nurseries will point them out. Plants are more suitable for northern gardens than those in the South due to poor tolerance on the part of many of the cultivars to heat- and stress-related diseases. Interestingly, one of the finest (if not the most eye-catching) phlox is the species itself. Bearing lavender flowers, reseeding itself and multiplying by root divisions, this indestructible native plant is much less susceptible to mildew and is a pleasure to have in all gardens, North and South.

Cultivars

Many colors are available, and while it is impossible to grow them all, here are a few of my favorites.

'Blue Ice' has a pinkish-blue eye in white flowers.

'Bright Eyes' bears pale pink blossoms with crimson eyes.

'Eva Cullum' has large heads of clean pink flowers with dark red eyes.

'Flamingo' produces large pink heads on compact plants.

'Franz Schubert' bears lilac flowers with darker star-shaped eyes.

'Fujiyama' ('Mt. Fuji') is one of the best white cultivars, bearing heavy 12- to 15-inch-long flower heads. One can see this snow-capped mountain from a distance.

'Norah Leigh' is grown for the variegated green-and-white leaves. The flowers are handsome, if not spectacular. Plants are difficult to locate, but we can hope they'll soon be in catalogs and garden centers.

'Sir John Falstaff' produces large flowers of salmon-pink.

'Starfire' has striking cherry red flowers that can be seen from across a football field.

SUBULATA (SUB-EW-LAH-TA)
Moss Phlox
Colors: Various
Zones: 2 to 8
○

Driving through the early spring landscape (late winter in the South) is a cinematographic adventure. Plants seem to cover hillsides, abandoned homesteads, and rock gardens throughout the land. Many stems with short, stiff foliage creep through and over the soil, with three to five flowers borne on each stem. Many of the older plantings are deep pink, but blue, red, and white flowers are also available. Unfortunately, little seed is produced and plants must be propagated by cuttings.

Cultivars

Dozens of cultivars have been offered, all of which are low growing and early flowering. Colors include blue ('Blue Hills'), purple ('Atropurpurea'), pink ('Coral Eye'), red ('Scarlet Flame'), and white ('White Delight').

'Candy Stripes' ('Tamanomagalei') has recently become available. The pink and white flowers are handsome in the spring.

Used as a cut flower and as a showy border plant, Physostegia virginiana *'Bouquet Rose' serves a dual purpose.*

PHYSOSTEGIA
(FIE-SO-STEE-GEE-A)
Obedient Plant

About a dozen species have been reported, but only *P. virginiana* is commonly offered.

VIRGINIANA
(VIR-JIN-EE-AYE-NA)
Obedient Plant
Color: Pink
Zones: 2 to 9
○

I have grown this species for years, and although plants have minds of their own, I have never

been disappointed. They are sufficiently cold hardy to grow in the northern states but also tolerate warm temperatures and high humidity. Flowers are lipped (like salvia) and are borne up the stem in a long spike. Generally flowers are pink, but rose and white selections are also available. Plants grow 3 to 4 feet tall and multiply by underground stems. Their ability to spread is well known before long the shovel becomes useful for removal rather than planting. Plants are not fussy as to soil; rich soils result in even more rampant growth than poor soils.

Cultivars

'Alba' bears off-white flowers two to three weeks earlier than the species.

'Bouquet Rose' produces deep rose-pink flowers and grows 3 to 4 feet tall in the South, 2 to 3 feet tall in the North.

'Summer Snow' bears white flowers.

'Variegata' is an interesting plant with green and white variegated foliage. The leaves are handsome and plants are grown more for the beauty of the foliage than the flowers.

'Vivid' is one of the most popular cultivars due to its bright pink flowers and dwarf habit. Some of the cultivars above require support, but 'Vivid' does not.

Platycodon grandiflorus 'Mariesii' is tall enough not to get lost in the garden but seldom needs support, even in the South.

PLATYCODON
(PLA - TEE - KO - DON)
Balloonflower
Zones: 3 to 8

The genus is represented by only one species, *P. grandiflorus*, but is found in gardens throughout the world. Balloonflower is a fun plant because of the way the flower buds expand to form "balloons." The balloons keep getting bigger and bigger until they finally pop open to reveal wonderful 2- to 3-inch-wide purple-blue flowers with rich purple veins. Provided with full sun, plants grow 2 to 2½ feet tall; a height of 3 feet is not uncommon in partial shade. They are one of the latest plants to emerge in the spring but they are also one of the most persistent from year to year. The combination of balloonflowers and tall yarrows, such as 'Coronation Gold' or 'Gold Plate', is particularly effective. Plants are usually self-supporting except in areas of hot summer nights, where they may flop over; selecting dwarf cultivars is a simple solution. They perform well in Zones 3 to 8 and are some of the lowest maintenance and most rewarding perennials available today.

Cultivars

'Albus' bears creamy white flowers with yellow veins.

'Apoyama' has violet-blue flowers on plants 15 to 18 inches tall.

'Komachi' is certainly different from other selections in that the buds expand normally but don't open. What is usually a seemingly endless wait for the flower is, in this case, just that.

'Mariesii' is one of the more common cultivars due to its dwarf habit. It grows 1 to 2 feet tall and is relatively self-supporting. Highly recommended for southern gardeners.

'Sentimental Blue' and 'Sentimental White' are dwarf cultivars (less than 18 inches tall) with lovely blue and white single flowers respectively.

'Plenus' produces double flowers. I think the single flower form of balloonflower is too handsome to mess up with a double flower.

Nursery people have been trying to select for bicolored flowers, usually blue and white, but the flowers have been uncooperatively unstable. Generally flowers revert to solid blue after the first two years. The search continues, and the stable bicolor will doubtless be available soon.

Lavender-blue flowers looking down over deep green foliage make Polemonium caeruleum *an excellent garden plant.*

POLEMONIUM
(PO-LEE-MO-nee-um)
Jacob's Ladder

Of the 50 to 60 species, only a few are available for American gardens. In general, most species do well in the western states, a few do well in the East, and one or two do well in the South. The flowers generally occur in various shades of blue, but white- and pink-flowering forms have been produced.

CAERULEUM (se-ru-LEE-um)
Jacob's Ladder
Color: Blue
Zones: 2 to 6

The leaves ascend the stem in such a manner as to suggest a ladder, supposedly associated with Jacob and climbed by all of us mortals. the leaves consist of up to 20 leaflets (compound leaf) and are handsome even without a flower. The light-blue-to-dark-blue flowers are borne at the top of the stems, each flower sporting bright yellow stamens. Plants perform well in full sun to partial shade in northern and western gardens. In the South, plants survive but flower poorly. Propagate by division after flowering by terminal cuttings, or seed.

Cultivars

'Album' bears white flowers that contrast well with the dark green foliage.

'Himalayanum' (var. *himalayanum*) has larger deeper blue flowers than the species and is more vigorous than the species.

REPTANS
(REP-tanz)
Creeping Polemonium
Color: Blue
Zones: 2 to 7

This eastern wildflower occurs through much of the eastern woodlands and midwestern plains. Seldom growing over 1 foot tall, plants produce fresh foliage, consisting of 7 to 15 leaflets, and light blue flowers. They reseed themselves well and quickly fill in areas with partial shade and moist conditions. A fine species for woodland gardens, both North and South.

POLYGONATUM
(PO-LIG-O-NAY-TUM)
Solomon's Seal

Classic native plants as well as species from Europe and Asia make up the genus of these beautiful garden plants. At one time, the pulverized

One of the finest early spring plants, Polygonatum odoratum *'Variegatum' brightens up even the shadiest area of the garden.*

roots were thought to be useful for healing broken bones and sealing wounds, but today the plants are included in the garden for their pendulous flowers and architectural qualities. Medicine has come a long way, thank goodness. The leaf orientation is delightful and the variegated forms are particularly showy. Most species are large and spread rapidly but *P. humile* (*P. falcatum*) is a marvelous, 9-inch species with greenish-white, bell-shaped flowers. A terrific little gem for the front of the garden.

CANALICULATUM
(KA-NAH-LICK-ew-lay-tum)
Giant Solomon's Seal
Color: White
Zones: 4 to 7

Truly giants in this genus, plants can grow to 7 feet tall and 4 feet wide; 4 to 6 feet in height is common. Not plants for the perennial border, a few by the edge of a moist woodland make an outstanding display. Plants perform best in moist, cool conditions and, once established, persist for many years. The yellowish-white flowers are borne under the leaf axils in groups of three to eight in the spring. A truly graceful woodland species. Plants are also offered as *P. giganteum* and *P. commutatum*; they are all the same.

ODORATUM (O-DO-RAH-tum)
Fragrant Solomon's Seal
Color: White
Zones: 3 to 8

This plant holds a special place in my garden. Although native to Europe and Asia, plants are outstanding in American gardens. I have tried a few of the green-leaf forms but they don't hold a candle to the variegated form 'Variegatum'. The foliage consists of soft green leaves edged in a broad strip of creamy white. The leaves jump out and light up a shady area. One to two fragrant white flowers with yellow-green skirts hang down from the leaf axils in the spring. I will not garden without it.

PRIMULA (PRIM-EU-LA)
Primrose

With well over 400 species, there are primroses for almost any garden. Primroses flower in the spring and are wonderful, handsome plants around ponds, or in rock gardens or moist, boggy areas. Although no species performs particularly well in hot climates or dry soils, not all primroses require cool, moist conditions to thrive. The most common primroses are the polyantha types, bred mainly for greenhouse pot crops; they work well only in benevolent summer climates found in the Northwest and Northeast. However, little-used primroses such as *P. kisoana*, *P. elatior*, *P. sieboldii*, and *P. tomassinii* are particularly heat tolerant and may be used far more, even in areas where primroses are seldom seen.

DENTICULATA (DEN-TIK-EW-LAH-TA)
Drumstick Primrose
Colors: Various
Zones: 4 to 7

In early spring, rounded heads consisting of dozens of small flowers arise over basal leaves. The stems are 4 to 6 inches long at flowering time and expand to about a foot in length after flowering. In North America, plants should be planted in the fall to allow for sufficient cooling; however, they do best in areas with sufficient snow cover. Plants are winter hardy to Zone 4 with snow cover (Zone 5 without) and summer hardy to about Zone 7. In the South, treat this primrose as an annual; plant in the fall and replace after flowering in the spring. Place in partially shaded areas with consistently moist soils. All cultivars are fairly easily propagated from seed.

Cultivars

'Alba' is a white-flowered form.

'Bressingham Beauty' is 8 to 12 inches tall with powdery blue flowers.

'Cashmere Beauty' ('Cashmeriana') bears wine-colored flowers over stems 12 inches tall.

A grouping of **Primula** *'Rowallane Hybrids' in a waterway or pond is guaranteed to take your breath away.*

'Karryann' produces light blue flowers and yellow variegated foliage.

Rhonsdorf Strain produces a mixture of flower colors on 12-inch-tall stems over compact plants.

'Rubin' ('Cashmeriana Rubin') produces red flowers and is similar in habit to 'Cashmere Beauty'.

JAPONICA (JA-PON-I-CA)
Japanese Primrose
Colors: Various
Zones: 5 to 7

Some of the most wonderful plants in the genus, *P. japonica* bears whorls of flowers on tall stems like lights on a candelabrum. The Japanese primroses are indeed members of a large group of primroses called "candelabras," of which *P. japonica* is probably the easiest to grow. The flower stems hold 2 to 6 whorls of flowers, each whorl consisting of 8 to 12 flowers each. Conditions for success are fairly critical; cool night temperatures and moist soils are recommended. This is an excellent plant for gardeners who love to try what standard gardening books say is impossible. Try Japanese primrose regardless of your location; you may be pleasantly surprised. (Plants can't read USDA hardiness maps.) One of the finest plantings of Japanese primroses may be found in Winterthur Gardens in Delaware. Most Japanese primroses may be raised from seed. Sow seed in moist peat or a 1:1 ratio of peat/perlite mixture. Provide warm temperatures (70 to 75 degrees Fahrenheit) and maintain humid conditions.

Cultivars

'Miller's Crimson' has wonderful deep red flowers.

'Postford White' bears many whorls of large white flowers, each with a contrasting yellow eye.

VULGARIS (VUL-GAH-RIS)
English Primrose
Color: Sulphur yellow
Zones: 4 to 8

An excellent and relatively available primrose in many areas of the country, plant bears nodding 1-inch-wide sulphur yellow flowers. I include this lovely primrose not only because of the handsome flowers but also because of the success I have had in the heat of a north Georgia climate. Being a *Primula* lover, I am always searching for low-frustration primroses (LFPs), those that succeed in an area where primroses are not supposed to be successful. The foliage of the English primrose remains dark green and healthy even through the summer in my zone. The vigorous growth is a nice change from watching my polyantha hybrids (polys) decline during the summer. Other heat-tolerant species (no primrose likes heat, but some tolerate it better than others) are not as easy to find, but *P. elatior* and *P. tomasinii* are also LFPs. *P. vulgaris* is so heat tolerant that plants reseed themselves in southeastern gardens.

Cultivars

'Rubra' bears deep red flowers and is a vigorous grower.

The spotted foliage of Pulmonaria *'Margery Fish' is striking.*

PULMONARIA
(PUL-MON-AIR-EE-A)
Jerusalem Cowslip, Lungwort

The spotted leaf of Jerusalem cowslip (*P. offici-nalis*) resembled a diseased lung to herbalists of the sixteenth and seventeenth centuries, and seemed an obvious choice to treat ailments of the lung. (If the patient didn't die of lung-related disease, he probably died from such a concoction.) Of the dozen species of lungwort, only about four are used with any degree of success in the garden. They are valuable for their handsome foliage, early flowers, and shade tolerance, and aren't used nearly enough by American gardeners. Plants may be propagated from seed or division after flowering.

ANGUSTIFOLIA
(ANG-GUS-TI-FO-LEE-A)
Blue Lungwort
Color: Blue
Zones: 2 to 7
◑

The bright blue flowers open as the unspotted leaves expand, and combine beautifully with some of the mid- to late-season daffodils. The flower buds emerge pink and go through a wonderful metamorphosis resulting in bright blue, drooping, funnel-shaped flowers. Plants grow about 12 inches tall and perform best in areas of acid soils. The foliage tends to wilt rapidly in the heat of the summer, but plants still do well in southern gardens.

Cultivars

'Azurea' bears handsome gentian blue flowers.

'Mawson's Variety' produces violet-blue flowers and is an outstanding cultivar.

'Munstead Blue' has dark blue flowers not unlike the species.

SACCHARATA (SA-KA-RAH-TA)
Bethlehem Sage
Color: Blue
Zones: 3 to 7
◑

The spotted foliage and blue flowers make this 9- to 18-inch-tall plant a prize for shaded and moist gardens. The leaves are about three times longer than wide and blotched with white spots. Plants are 9 to 18 inches tall. The pink flower buds give way to blue flowers in the spring; however, the foliage is sufficiently handsome even if plants don't produce abundant flowers. While the foliage is pleasant in the spring, leaves look particularly wretched if consistently allowed to wilt. It is essential to plant Bethlehem sage in areas where moisture is available.

Cultivars

'Boughton Blue' has silvery gray blotches with clear blue flowers.

Uncommon but not rare, Santolina virens *provides showy yellow flowers over bright green foliage.*

SANTOLINA (SAN-TO-LEEN-A)
Lavender Cotton

About eight species of lavender cotton occur, but the most popular is common lavender cotton, sporting the almost-unpronounceable name of *Santolina chamaecyparissus* (KA-MIE-SIP-PA-RIS-IS). Say that one quickly! The foliage is gray-green and aromatic, and in well-drained soils and bright light it takes on a white sheen. Plants are used as edging or as foils for harsher colors in the border. The flowers resemble little yellow globes; they don't really add anything to the plant's appearance. Winter hardiness north of Zone 5 and summer hardiness south of Zone 8 are questionable. *Santolina* performs well in areas of high humidity and frequent afternoon rains only if drainage is excellent. Place in full sun in the North; partial shade is tolerated in the South.

Other Species

Santolina virens, green lavender cotton, has bright green foliage and is exceptional when sited correctly. Good drainage, morning sun, and a relatively dry climate are to its liking. The yellow flowers are a pleasing contrast to the fresh foliage.

Large lavender-blue flowers of Scabiosa caucasica *'Butterfly Blue' stand beautifully in a container in a northeastern garden.*

SCABIOSA (SKAB-EE-O-SA)
Scabious, Pincushion Flower

The easiest to grow species in this group of plants is scabious (*S. caucasica* [KAW-KA-SI-CA]), with summer flowers in various shades of blue or white. The pastel blue flowers appear during the heat of the summer and contrast well with the many bright yellow daisies of July and August. Growing 18 to 24 inches tall, they can be woven into the front or middle of the garden. They may be carefully divided in late summer and fall after three or four years but plants aren't at all invasive. Seed propagation also is useful for the species and some of the cultivars.

Cultivars

Var. *alba* is a creamy white-flowered cultivar that comes true from seed. The plants grow 18 to 24 inches tall.

'Blue Perfection' bears fringed lavender-blue flowers and grows about 2 feet tall.

'Butterfly Blue' is a relatively recent selection with excellent blue flowers and compact (15 to 18 inches tall) habit. Flowering continues throughout the season.

'Compliment' ('Kompliment'), is 20 to 24 inches tall with large dark lavender flowers.

'Fama' produces lavender-blue flowers with silver centers on compact stems 18 inches tall.

House's hybrids are a popular mix of white and blue shades.

'Loddon White' and 'Bressingham White' bear large creamy white flowers on plants 2½ to 3 feet tall.

'Moonstone' produces light lavender-blue flowers on 18- to 24- inch plants. Its pastel shade and compact growth makes this an excellent cultivar.

A difficult plant to beat for late summer and fall flowering, Sedum 'Autumn Joy' is popular for good reason.

SEDUM (SEED-um)
Stonecrop

A tremendous number of species occur, most of which have been popularized by rock gardeners and alpine enthusiasts. While many of the 500 or more species are low growing, a number are also upright vigorous plants useful as specimens.

ACRE (A-KER)
Golden Stonecrop
Color: Yellow
Zones: 3 to 8

A wonderful, although invasive, mat-forming groundcover, *S. acre* is used between stepping stones, hanging over walls and ledges, and to cover large areas in a mantle of yellow and green. Although plants do well in full sun, they obediently cover the ground if provided with partial shade; the flowers, however, are reduced in shade. When in full bloom, the showy yellow flowers can be a beacon to any wayward wanderer. Perhaps, for this reason, the common name of "Welcome-home-husband-though-never-so-drunk" is appropriate. Be careful to plant it away from other low-growing plants, because it will eventually smother everything in its path. Thin the planting every two to three years; little other maintenance is necessary.

Cultivars

'Aureum' bears a golden tint on the young leaves and is particularly attractive in the spring. In warm climates, the tint disappears in the heat of the summer.

'Elegans' has foliage with a silver rather than yellow tint. A lovely cultivar, but one that eventually loses its distinctive hue. Both of the above cultivars are less vigorous than the species.

'AUTUMN JOY'
Autumn Joy Sedum
Color: Pink
Zones: 3 to 10

○

I have admired this hybrid from Montreal to Orlando and to San Diego, and if one is searching for a foolproof plant for a sunny area, one need look no farther. 'Autumn Joy', originally introduced from Germany as 'Herbstfreude', grows about 18 to 24 inches tall. It begins to flower in mid- to late August and continues for many weeks. 'Autumn Joy' combines well with *Rudbeckia* 'Goldsturm', fall-flowering salvias, and late-season coneflowers. These plants are almost indestructible, withstanding abuse from drought, humidity, cold, heat, and my dog, not necessarily in that order. The key to success is full sun; without it, plants grow too tall and require support. They may be divided anytime, but a large planting is particularly attractive. From handsome emerging clumps in the spring to attractive seed heads in the fall, this plant has something for everyone.

KAMTSCHATICUM
(KAMT-SHA-ti-cum)
Kamchatka Stonecrop
Color: Orange-yellow
Zones: 3 to 8

○

Growing only about 8 inches tall, this spreader produces small orange-yellow flowers at the end of each stem, followed by attractive, small red fruit. Provided with full sun and good drainage,

plants are handsome and can be breathtaking. Flowers appear in early to midsummer and once flowering has occurred, long straggly stems may be cut back to 6 to 8 inches long. If cut back, however, no fruit will form. Plants are hardy from Zones 3 to 7.

Cultivars

Var. *floriferum*, as the name suggests, bears more flowers than the species. 'Weihenstephaner Gold' is a compact floriferous form covered with golden yellow flowers in late May. Beautiful in well-drained soils.

'Variegatum' leaves feature a broad white band.

* TERNATUM (TER-NA-TUM)
Whorled Stonecrop
Color: White
Zones: 4 to 8

Native to the eastern United States, this 2- to 6-inch-tall mat-former is one of my favorite understated wildflowers. The gray-green leaves are whorled about pale green stems and remain evergreen in mild climates. The white starlike flowers appear in early spring and are effective for two to four weeks. Tolerant of shade but not happy with wet conditions, plants are particularly effective on rocky slopes and steep banks. They root readily along the stem and may be divided anytime.

A wonderful native plant, Silene polypetala *rewards the gardener who provides shade and consistent moisture.*

SILENE (SI-LEE-KNEE)
Campion

Numerous species occur, and some of the most wonderful are wildflowers in our backyards. The native fire pink (*Silene virginica*) lights up the Smoky Mountains of North Carolina to the Alleghenies of New York. The pink flowers of Carolina pink (*S. caroliniana*) and some of its variants can be found as far north as Ohio. One of the most beautiful of all is indisputably the fringed campion, *S. polypetala*.

POLYPETALA (PAH-LEE-PET-A-LA)
Fringed Campion
Color: Pink
Zones: 6 to 8

Plants grow 4 to 6 inches tall and spread well where the site is to their liking. The evergreen foliage contrasts well with the lavender-pink fringed petals that emerge in mid- to late spring. Flowers persist for three to four weeks and inspire continuous comment. Do not allow plants to dry out, and beware because they don't tolerate heavy soils or poor drainage. Although fringed campion is on the State of Georgia Endangered Species List, tissue-culture techniques and other propagation methods have brought large numbers of this plant into production.

Other Species

Dr. Jim Ault, while working on a postdoctorate at the University of Georgia, crossed *S. polypetala* with *S. virginica*. The resulting hybrid is known as *S.* × 'Jim Ault'. Plants are more vigorous than *S. polypetala*, and the flowers are deep pink with handsome fringed petals. A plant with excellent garden potential although difficult to locate.

Variegated foliage and bright yellow flowers make Sisyrinchium striatum 'Aunt May' well worth the time to locate it.

SISYRINCHIUM (SI-SEE-RING-EE-UM)
Blue-eyed Grass

While numerous species are native to the United States, only a few have found their way into American gardens. Although the genus belongs to the iris family, plants are referred to as "grass" because of the grasslike foliage of our native *S. angustifolia*. One of the most ornamental species is the variegated form of Argentine blue-eyed grass (*S. striatum* 'Variegata', 'Aunt May').

STRIATUM (STREYE-A-TUM)
Argentine Blue-eyed Grass
Color: Yellow
Zones: 4 to 7
○

The species bears 9 to 12 creamy yellow flowers on upright spikes and attains a height of 18 to 24 inches. The back of each flower has a purple stripe, and the center is a darker yellow than the rest of the flower. The foliage is similar to that of the bearded iris, and when not in flower, the two can be confused. The leaves of the variegated form 'Aunt May' have creamy white margins surrounding the gray-green centers and are especially attractive. Place in full sun for best variegation.

The abundant primrose-yellow flowers of ✕ Solidaster luteus are a wonderful change from the many strident yellow flowers of summer.

× *SOLIDASTER*
(SO-LI-DAST-er)
Solidaster
Zones: 3 to 9

The taxonomists are still debating the origin of this intergeneric cross between *Aster* and *Solidago* (goldenrod). Some authorities even dismiss the genus and relegate it to *Solidago*. Regardless of origin, a few cultivars are useful for the garden and should be more widely used. In general, plants of *Solidaster luteus* are 2 to 3 feet tall and combine attributes of each genus.

Cultivars

'Lemore' has primrose yellow flowers similar to those of another fine cultivar, 'Super'. The flowers are more handsome than either aster or goldenrod and open in mid- to late summer. Flowers may also be cut and en-joyed indoors for at least 10 days before declining. Unfortunately, plants are susceptible to rust, particularly in the East and Midwest. Cut back plants after flowering and divide in early spring or fall. Place in full sun and do not let them be crowded by other plants. Natural ventilation reduces the incidence of rust.

STACHYS (STA-KIS)
Betony
Zones: 4 to 7

Of the many possible garden species in the genus, it is a hairy, gray-leaved one that gardeners have come to embrace. Known as lamb's ears because of its soft, furry oval leaves, the plant is cultivated as *S. byzantina* (BI-ZAN-TEEN-A). The

The gray fuzzy leaves of lamb's ears, Stachys byzantina, *are useful to soften the contours of a flower bed.*

gray color and the pillowlike feel of the foliage can be found throughout gardens in America, but unbeknownst to many southern gardeners, it performs poorly south of Zone 7. Plants look best in the spring but the hairy foliage tends to trap water, resulting in leaf rot and melt-out if late afternoon rains are commonplace. Melt-out is a polite way of saying that the plants rot in the middle by leaving a few poor hangers-on around the outside. Definitely a sad demise for a handsome plant. Although some disagree, I think the flowers detract from the foliage and add nothing to the plant (and even less to the overall garden effect). With my handy horticultural thumbnail, I make quick work of all interloping blooms. Moist but well-drained soils are ideal. Always water in the morning to allow foliage to dry out during the day. If possible, use subirrigation rather than overhead watering to reduce leaf melt-out.

Cultivars

'Silver Carpet' produces carpets of silvery foliage but doesn't produce flowers. This is my favorite.

'Sheila Macqueen' ('Cotton Boll') is not very different from the species but does have slightly larger leaves on a more compact plant.

* STOKESIA (STOKS-EE-A)
Stoke's Aster
Zones: 5 to 8

The blue flowers of the native plant *S. laevis* may be found in the southern United States from South Carolina to Florida and west to Louisiana. The leaves are evergreen when not covered by snow and begin to grow vigorously as soon as temperatures warm up in the spring. Daisylike 2- to 3-inch-wide flowers begin to appear in early June in my Georgia garden and continue for three to four weeks. Plants tolerate full sun but filtered light is best. Avoid waterlogged soils. Plants are persistent; mine have been with me for eight years and show no signs of decline.

Persistent lavender-blue flowers of Stokesia laevis *'Blue Danube' reappear consistently each year in late spring and early summer.*

Woodland gardens brighten up with the arrival of the bright yellow flowers of Stylophorum diphyllum *in the spring.*

Cultivars

'Alba' has creamy white flowers that contrast well with the dark foliage.

'Blue Danube' bears large lavender-blue flowers on plants 12 to 18 inch tall.

'Klaus Jelitto' is a relatively new introduction to the American market. Large (3-inch-diameter) lavender flowers are produced on compact 15- to 18-inch plants. Appears to be an excellent cultivar.

'Silver Moon' produces silvery white flowers a little larger than those of 'Alba' and equally handsome.

'Wyoming' bears many deep blue flowers on compact plants.

STYLOPHORUM
(STY-LAH-FOR-UM)
Celandine Poppy
Zones: 4 to 9

The richness of our native flora is often overlooked. One only has to produce a few plants of *S. diphyllum* (celandine, or wood, poppy) to quickly make converts out of disbelievers. Native to much of eastern North America, these plants make a wonderful display in and around woodlands and ponds. A well-designed woodland garden is a joy, and one of the finest I have visited belongs to Ed and Donna Lambert in Athens, Georgia. An early spring stroll along the narrow, natural paths brings you eye to eye with ferns, bluebells, gingers, rues, jack-in-the-pulpits, and some of the finest, most vigorous celandine poppies to be found anywhere. Their garden is a testament to their enthusiasm and effort. When I take my students there, they leave as wildflower believers.

In late winter and early spring, the gray-green compound leaves emerge through the soil and drag the first of the bright yellow flowers with them. Plants grow 12 to 18 inches tall and bear dozens of flowers. The foliage often disappears by late June or July, but if plants are grown in moist areas, the foliage doesn't decline until the fall. Under good conditions, plants self-sow and seedlings arise throughout the garden. We should all be so lucky. Plants may be divided after flowering, but care must be taken not to damage the thick rootstock.

One of my favorites of the genus, Thalictrum rochebrunianum *provides fountains of flowers in late spring and summer.*

THALICTRUM (THA-LIK-TRUM)
Meadow Rue

A most underused and underappreciated genus, *Thalictrum* has something for everyone. From native woodlanders, such as early meadow rue (*T. dioicum*) to tall yellow-flowered European species, such as dusty meadow rue (*T. speciosissimum*), gardeners have a wide choice of handsome plants. In general, plants have coarse compound fernlike foliage and great puffs of airy flowers.

AQUILEGIFOLIUM
(A-KWI-LEEG-I-FO-LEE-UM)
Columbine Meadow Rue
Colors: Pink and lavender
Zones: 5 to 7

The blue-green leaves are so similar to those of columbine that the two are often confused; however, the flowers of meadow rue are entirely different. They have no petals, and it is the long, protruding lilac stamens that provide the ornamental value of the flowers. Many flowers occur together in clusters that look like big powder puffs. Flowering begins as early as late April in my garden (about a month later in Zone 5 gardens), and persists for two to three weeks. Plants grow 2 to 3 feet tall (up to 5 feet tall where they are joyously happy) and combine well with early iris. An excellent rue for both North and South, it is heat- and somewhat drought-tolerant. Support may be required, particularly in rich soils. Place in partial shade in well-drained soil.

Cultivars

'Album' bears creamy white flowers on plants 3 to 4 feet tall. The flowers contrast well with the blue-green foliage.

'Dwarf Purple' has lilac flowers and differs from the species only in its smaller (2-foot-tall) stature.

'Roseum' bears light pink to pale rose flowers.

'Thundercloud' produces deep purple flowers with larger flower heads than the species.

'White Cloud' has larger, cleaner white flowers than 'Album'.

ROCHEBRUNIANUM
(ROSH-BROON-EE-AYE-NUM)
Lavender Mist
Color: Lavender
Zones: 4 to 8

An excellent, vigorous plant with strong, erect stems and smooth fernlike leaves. The stems are strong and unlikely to require support. Rose-lavender flowers with yellow stamens are borne in loose sprays atop 4-foot-tall stems in late spring and early summer. A terrific plant for American gardeners, it has now become much more widely available. Provide it with a little shade, keep it in moist, rich soil away from hot afternoon sun and enjoy your lavender mist with a little Irish Mist—a wonderful combination.

Appearing in early spring, the yellow pea-like flowers of Thermopsis caroliniana *catch everyone's attention.*

THERMOPSIS (THER-MOP-SIS)
False Lupine

Although about 20 species occur, less than a handful are cultivated to any extent. One of the best is the southern, or Carolina, lupine, *T. caroliniana*, native to the eastern United States, although others are equally ornamental. The yellow lupine-like flowers are held in compact, erect 6- to 12-inch-long racemes on plants 3 feet tall. The blue-green leaves are divided into 3 leaflets each and are handsome even before flowers appear. However, foliage may decline and need to be cut back after flowering has finished, particularly in areas with hot summers. Plant in full sun in ordinary garden soil. Plants may be divided. Although I have had some problems, Barry Glick of Sunshine Nurseries in West Virginia reports that small divisions, taken in the spring with a few roots, then dipped in Dip and Grow hormone solution, were 100 percent successful.

Cultivars

'Album' bears creamy white flowers, grows 2 to 3 feet tall and is most ornamental.

Other Species

T. montana (mountain thermopsis), native from the Rocky Mountains to Washington, is similar to its eastern cousin. Leaf shape, plant height, and flower density differ somewhat, and mountain thermopsis is not as tolerant of heat and humidity as Carolina thermopsis.

An outstanding new cultivar of Tiarella cordifolia, *'Oakleaf',
provides handsome foliage and pink flowers.*

* *TIARELLA* (TEE-A-REL-A)
Foamflower
Zones: 3 to 8

A marvelous native plant, foamflower offers low
maintenance, vigorous growth, handsome flowers, and ornamental foliage. About six species
occur, but Allegheny foamflower (*T. cordifolia*
[KOR-DI-FO-LEE-A]) and its variants are available as nursery-grown plants (do not gather from
the wild). The 3- to 4-inch-wide heart-shaped
leaves are dark purple in the fall and winter. As
the weather warms, pink-tinged flower buds arise
to give way to starry, creamy white flowers on
3- to 4-inch-long flower stems. Plants are stoloniferous and can be invasive, although I keep hop-
ing my few plants would be more like Atilla and
conquer more territory. They perform well in
Zones 3 to 8 and are effective with trilliums,
early phlox, and Solomon's seal. Plant in a shady,
moisture-retentive area. They don't like being
dried out. If necessary, incorporate sufficient organic matter to enrich the soil.

Cultivars

Ssp. *collina* (*T. wherryi*), Wherry's foamflower, is similar but not stoloniferous. For
gardeners experiencing invasive problems
with Allegheny foamflower, this is a more
well-behaved form. Feel free to send me any
of your invading hordes.

'Oakleaf' is beautiful with indented leaves
and long spires of flowers. Magnificent.

TRICYRTIS (TRI-SER-TIS)
Toad Lily

I think a gardener is truly bitten by the plant
bug when he becomes enamored with toad lilies.
A comparison that comes to mind is this: One
must pass through basic arithmetic and algebra
to appreciate the intricacies of calculus. Toad lilies are the higher mathematics of herbaceous perennials. Walking through Charles Cresson's

With flowers of light to deep purple, Tricyrtis formosana *is
easy to grow and much underused.*

magnificent garden near Philadelphia, I discover species and varieties of toad lilies I never knew existed. If his toad lilies are good, you know the rest of the garden is outstanding. *T. macropoda, T. dilitata, T. perfoliata,* and *T. macrantha* are but a few species worth trying. Fortunately, some of these species are becoming available, but they are not particularly easy to find.

FORMOSANA (FOR-MO-SAH-NA)
(syn. *T. stolonifera*)
Formosa Toad Lily
Color: Lilac
Zones: 4 to 8

Probably the best and easiest species to work with, Formosa toad lily bears many lilac flowers with interesting interior markings. Flowers occur at the top of the many stems and also in the upper leaf axils. Plants are less susceptible to disease and insects than common toad lily (*T. hirta*), and are more vigorous. They spread by stolons and form large clumps in two to three years. While I don't consider them invasive, I always have a few offsets to share with others. (The only problem you may have is persuading friends into accepting anything with the name of an amphibian.) Provide full sun to partial shade and well-drained soil. Toad lilies are wonderful with blue velvet sage (*Salvia leucantha*).

HIRTA (HIR-TA)
Common Toad Lily
Color: Lilac
Zones: 4 to 8

Lilac flowers form in the leaf axils along the 2- to 3-foot-long arching stems in late summer and early fall. The flowers have a lilac-to-white background often with purple spots throughout.

Plants are not stoloniferous but can form large clumps. They appear more susceptible to fungal and insect attacks than *T. formosana* and haven't performed as well in my garden. They prefer cooler, drier weather and I have seen lovely specimens in gardens around Philadelphia, Seattle, and Portland.

Cultivars

Var. *alba* has white flowers with pink stamens.

'Miyazaki' has graceful arching stems with axillary flowers that open in the fall. Plants are more vigorous than the species and I have been more successful with it than with the species.

*TRILLIUM (TRIL-LEE-UM)
Trillium

All the world loves a trillium, and unfortunately, half the world wants to dig them from the wild.

The epitome of the eastern American native plant, Trillium grandiflorum *provides unequalled beauty in a shady woodland garden.*

The trillium is the epitome of the American wild-flower, on a par with the gunfighters of the Old West. *T. grandiflorum* (great white trillium) has been abused to the point that many native stands have gone the way of those gunfighters. No more digging, please. Trilliums are grouped botanically by the presence or absence of a flower stem, known as the pedicel. Both groups consist of well-known handsome species.

GRANDIFLORUM
(GRAND-I-FLOR-UM)
Great White Trillium
Colors: White, pink
Zones: 4 to 8

The most beloved trillium, it is known as wake-robin, showy trillium, snow trillium, wood lily, great white trillium, and trinity flower. The number of common names is a tribute to its geographic range, from Minnesota to Quebec and Missouri to Florida. Plants emerge in the spring. The wavy light green leaves may be 3 to 4 inches wide and plants grow 12 to 18 inches tall. The white 2- to 3-inch-wide flowers are attached to the stem by a pedicel and consist of three flaring sepals. As they mature, the flowers often fade to a soft pink. Round berries are produced after flowering. Plants go dormant in mid- to late summer, depending on temperature and water. They are well suited for northern and southern climes, but all benefit from shady, consistently moist conditions. Place copious amounts of organic matter in the planting area. Many nurseries offer propagated trilliums at a reasonable price and there is no longer any excuse for digging them from the wild. Trilliums purchased from a nursery have a far greater chance of flourishing in the garden than those pillaged from the woods.

Cultivars

Var. *roseum* may simply be a more intensely colored form of the species or truly a separate variety. The flowers are deeper pink and magnificent.

'Flore-pleno' bears double flowers. While I am not particularly fond of double-flowered plants, this grows on me and I find it interesting and handsome. Difficult to find and relatively expensive.

SESSILE (SESS-AISLE)
Sessile Trillium
Color: Purple
Zones: 5 to 8

As the species name implies, the flowers sit atop the main stem, not attached to a separate flower stem. The foliage usually is mottled with purple and the petals are purplish to green. Fascinating, but hard to love. Other sessile trilliums include the yellow *T. luteum* and the purplish *T. cuneatum* (toad trillium). To the trillium lover, there is no such thing as a mediocre trillium. Plant in shady, moist conditions but don't allow soil to become waterlogged.

Flowering in the spring or early summer, the easy-to-grow Verbascum phoeniceum *puts on a handsome display.*

VERBASCUM (VER-BAS-CUM)
Mullein

From weeds to wonders, mullein has it all. The roadside weed, towering over Hondas and Fiestas, is difficult to envision in one's garden; however, more civilized and ornamental brethren occur and are fine garden plants.

OLYMPICUM (O-LIM-PI-CUM)
Olympic Mullein
Color: Yellow
Zones: 6 to 8
○

The ornamental value of this species lies in the whitish gray, woolly, 6- to 8-inch-long leaves. Even when plants aren't in flower, the foliage is outstanding and complements almost all plants in the garden. Plants can grow to 5 feet or taller and 4 feet across, so this is not a plant to shoehorn into a small garden site. The 1-inch-wide yellow flowers open in early summer and persist for six to eight weeks. Gangly and curious, these plants can hardly be called pretty, but they change constantly over the season and surely make a garden more personal. Although technically a biennial, if placed in full sun in relatively well-drained soil, plants reseed and return for many years.

PHOENICEUM (FOY-NEE-SEE-UM)
Purple Mullein
Colors: Various
Zones: 5 to 7
○

Dark green rosettes of crinkled, shallowly lobed foliage give rise to long inflorescences of 1-inch-wide flowers in late spring. Plants and flowers display considerable variation and flowers may be purple, rose, red, or white. Full sun is best but plants tolerate partial shade. They are at their best in well-drained soils and where extremes of temperature are uncommon, such as the Northwest. Plants have not performed particularly well in the South. Flowers are fleeting, blooming for about two weeks, then disappearing. Propagation by seed is not difficult.

The deep purple flowers of Verbena *'Homestead Purple' combine beautifully with the yellow of* Oenothera perennis *in this Georgia garden.*

VERBENA (VER-BEEN-A)
Verbena

Verbena are gaining popularity every year as additional species and cultivars find their way to the garden grounds. The annual bedding verbena (*V.* × *hybrida*) is a stew of various species and provides season-long color, particularly in the northern states. Many species are native to South America but have naturalized along roadsides so much that they seem as though they are ours. Their heritage of warmer climates makes them somewhat tender in northern states where cold hardiness may be a problem.

BONARIENSIS
(BO-NAH-REE-EN-SIS)
Brazilian Verbena
Color: Lavender-purple
Zones: 7 to 10

○

In my mind, this is one of the most useful verbenas for the garden and container. Plants stand 3 to 4 feet tall and the upright, hairy, square stems are like purple-topped soldiers standing shoulder to shoulder at attention. Each lavender-purple flower is only ¼ inch across, but the entire flower head is 1½ to 2 inches wide. Plants should be planted toward the middle of the garden and may be used as center plantings in large patio containers. One of the finest container plantings I have seen was a 2- to 3-foot-tall multistemmed plant of *V. bonariensis* surrounded by petunias cascading down the sides, an excellent design idea from Post Properties of Atlanta. The planting demonstrates that creative people make good plants look even better. Place in full sun; shade results in excessively tall plants and powdery mildew may become a problem.

CANADENSIS (KAN-A-DEN-SIS)
Clump Verbena
Colors: Various
Zones: 6 to 10
◯

Native west to Colorado, south to Mexico, and along the eastern seaboard from Virginia to Florida, clump verbena is often sold as an annual, although it returns in the southern half of the country. Numerous cultivars are becoming available but the parentage is confused at best. The ground-hugging stems may become quite long and may be cut back severely anytime. Plant in full sun, preferably on a mild slope, where good drainage can be assured. They are also excellent as container plants as they'll obligingly spill down the sides. The major problems with this species, as with all low-growing forms, are spider mites, and root rot resulting from poor drainage.

Cultivars

All of these cultivars are hybrids with *V. canadensis*. More seem to appear every year.

'Abbeville' ('Lavender') produces handsome lavender-pink flowers. Selected by Goodness Grows nursery in Lexington, Georgia. Exceptionally handsome.

'Carousel' bears blue-and-white flowers at the ends of cascading stems.

'Gene Cline', named after plantsman Gene Cline of Canton, Georgia, is 6 to 9 inches tall with deep rose flowers.

'Homestead Purple', selected by the University of Georgia, is a vigorous, very early deep-purple-flowering form. One of the finest cultivars for season-long flowering, particularly on a slope.

'Pink Parfait' bears pink-and-white flowers. Handsome, but not as vigorous as some of the other cultivars.

RIGIDA (RI-GI-DA)
(syn. *V. venosa*)
Rigid Verbena
Color: Purple
Zones: 7 to 10
◯

Another species that has found happiness along the roadsides and pastures of America, rigid verbena is native to South America, from Brazil to Argentina. Although perennial in southern areas of the country, plants produce tuberous roots, like those of dahlias, which may be lifted and stored over the winter in northern states. Plants can become invasive and may reseed heavily where conditions are to their liking. Plants resemble miniature *V. bonariensis*, standing 12 to 18 inches tall, but are much hairier, with stems rough to the touch. Place in full sun and well-drained soil.

Cultivars

'Flame', likely a hybrid between *V. rigida* and *V. canadensis*, is 6 inches tall and bears many scarlet flowers.

Var. *lilacina* bears many handsome lilac-blue flowers. I have seen beautiful plantings in the Southeast and as far north as the Royal Botanical Gardens in Hamilton, Ontario.

'Polaris' is particularly outstanding, producing light lavender flowers on 1½- to 2-foot-tall stems. Plants self-sow under favorable conditions and can be a nuisance.

VERONICA (VE-RON-I-CA)
Speedwell

Of the 250 species in the genus, a dozen or so have found their way into the garden. Most have blue flowers, but white and rose flowers may also be found. Ranging in height from creeping to 4-foot-tall species, *Veronica* can add beauty to any garden. Full sun and well-drained soils are their only demands.

Loaded with flowers, Veronica spicata *'Blue Fox' is wonderful in a sunny garden.*

ALPINA (AL-PINE-A)
Alpine Speedwell
Color: Lavender
Zones: 3 to 7

According to the specific name, alpine speedwell should be at home only in alpinelike conditions, but it performs wonderfully well from Montreal to north Georgia. Plants grow only 6 to 9 inches tall and prefer to be near the front of the garden in a sunny well-drained site. Provide afternoon shade in the South; full sun is preferable in the North. White flowers occur on 'Alba', the best garden form, which combines the vigor of the species with the beauty of clean white flowers. Remove old flower stalks to ensure continued flowering.

Cultivars

'Goodness Grows' is an excellent long-flowering hybrid between *V. alpina* 'Alba' and *V. spicata*. The long violet-blue racemes contrast well with the rich green foliage. It arose as a volunteer at Goodness Grows Nursery, Lexington, Georgia.

LONGIFOLIA (LONG-GI-FO-LEE-A)
Long-leaf Veronica
Color: Lilac-blue
Zones: 4 to 7

A favorite of gardeners for years because of its vigorous habit and ease of growth, long-leaf veronica bears lilac-blue flowers in early summer on 2- to 3-foot-tall plants. The individual flowers are only about ¼ inch wide but are densely arranged on long straight racemes. All veronicas make excellent cut flowers, and this species and its various cultivars are used commercially in the cut-flower trade. Zone 7 or 8 is the southern limit; farther south they tend to become lank and leggy and require persistent shearing. I have had great success with some selections in our cut-flower trials at the University of Georgia. Plants consistently return each spring as far north as Zone 4, particularly if nature has provided some snow cover; cold snowless winters may result in a few losses. Plants will flower again in late summer and fall if cut back. Fertilize lightly, if at all.

Cultivars

'Alba' bears white flowers and is about 1½ feet tall.

'Blue Giant' is just that, growing as tall as 3½ feet and producing lavender-blue flowers.

'Foerster's Blue' stands 1½ to 2 feet tall and bears deep blue flowers for many weeks in the summer.

'Schneeriesen' has many creamy white flowers on plants 2 feet tall. It has performed well in our cut-flower trials and is a good garden plant as well.

Var. *subsessilis* may be a separate species (*V. subsessilis*) but remains one of the best garden forms. Bushy plants grow only about 2 feet tall and bear many blue flowers throughout the season.

'Sunny Border Blue' may be a hybrid, but arose at Sunny Border Nursery in Kensington, Connecticut. This outstanding plant has candles of lavender-blue flowers on plants 2 feet tall. It has outperformed most other veronicas in my garden, even tolerating partial shade and my dog.

SPICATA (SPEE-KAH-TA)
Spiked Speedwell
Colors: Various
Zones: 3 to 8
○

A favorite garden plant, spiked speedwell is more dwarf than other upright veronicas, better behaved and available in many colors with exciting names. The flowers are held in racemes (as in other veronicas) and they last for a six- to seven-week period in late spring and summer. Provide full sun in the North, afternoon shade in the South, and well-drained soils. Plants are generally 18 to 24 inches tall and suitable for the second tier of seats behind the front-row sitters in the border.

Cultivars

'Alba' is similar to the species but with white flowers.

'Baccarole' bears rosy pink flowers, gray-green leaves, and stands about 15 inches tall.

'Blue Fox' produces lavender-blue flowers on plants 15 to 20 inches tall.

'Blue Spires' has deep metallic green foliage and dense blue flowers on plants 12 to 18 inches tall. Plants were excellent in our trials, flowering for about four weeks in summer.

'Heidekind' is only 8 to 10 inches tall with rose-pink flowers. Less cold hardy than most other cultivars, it may not return north of Zone 5.

'Red Fox' has deep rosy red flowers and glossy green foliage. It stands 15 to 24 inches high and is a vigorous grower. Cut back old blooms to encourage additional flowering.

'Romiley Purple' bears deep violet-blue flowers on stems 2 feet tall. Difficult to locate in the United States.

'Snow White' has branching white flower spikes on stems 18 inches tall.

TEUCRIUM (TEWK-REE-um)
Hungarian Speedwell
Color: Deep blue
Zones: 3 to 8
○

Hungarian speedwell is a low-growing species easily confused with other ground huggers in the same genus. Some taxonomists have made the species a subspecies of *V. austrica*; other, more simple-minded people like myself list it separately to avoid confusion. The lovely blue flowers arise from the many leaf axils, and plants can be smothered with flowers from May through July for weeks on end. In areas with cool night temperatures, the richness of the flower color is legend. Cut back plants hard after flowering, particularly in the South, to encourage additional growth and flowering. Provide full sun in the North; partial shade is tolerated but not necessary in the South.

Cultivars

'Blue Fountain' has dense blue flowers on rather tall (up to 24-inch) plants.

'Crater Lake Blue' is one of the best cultivars, bearing rich blue flowers over dense, matlike growth.

'Knallblau' forms dense mats of light blue flowers.

'Royal Blue' is about 12 inches tall and produces many deep blue flowers.

'Shirley Blue' is 6 to 8 inches tall with short dark blue flower stems.

❋ VERONICASTRUM
(VE-RO-NI-KAS-TRUM)
Culver's Root
Color: Lilac-blue
Zones: 3 to 7
○

The only native species in this genus, *V. virginicum*, is sometimes sold by its old name, *Veronica virginica*. Although somewhat similar to *Veronica*, the leaves are whorled rather than opposite, and

A much-underused native plant, Culver's root, Veronicastrum virginicum *'Album', provides classic lines in the summer.*

plants are up to 3 feet tall, with a totally different look in the garden. Culver's root is native to the eastern United States and an overlooked native plant for American gardens. Flowers are sometimes blue to lilac-blue, but the most common form is the white-flowered 'Album'. Provide full sun to afternoon shade and well-drained soils. I have lost some due to winter rains and poor drainage.

Cultivars

'Album' has creamy white flowers on plants 3 feet tall. An excellent garden plant and cut flower, it has performed well in my garden and in the cut-flower trials for years. Much prettier than the species.

'Roseum' has rose-pink flowers and is more difficult to locate than 'Album'.

The large lavender and white flowers of Viola pedata *'Artist's Palette' are a far cry from the small flowers of the woodland species.*

VIOLA (VIE-O-LA)
Violet

The saying, "One man's weed is another man's treasure" is nowhere more true than in the case of violets. Some of my most treasured little plants are violets. *V. labradorica* (Labrador violet), *V. odorata* (sweet violet) and *V. pedata* (bird's-foot violet) are but three that come quickly to mind. However, no weed is more widespread and downright omnipotent than the violet-flowered *V. cucullata*, the marsh blue violet. Although the flowers are handsome and the plants tough, seedlings appear everywhere in spring and if not removed throw a party and invite all their friends. For every dark cloud, however, there is a silver lining. I now use the discarded plants to line my paths through the oak woods. Even with almost no light and constant abuse, they flourish. And while I curse them, I would hate to be too efficient in removing them—after all, I could be cursed with *Houttuynia* or something equally obnoxious.

LABRADORICA (LAB-RA-DOOR-I-KA)
Labrador Violet
Color: Violet
Zones: 3 to 8

Small, dark-green-to-purple leaves set off the handsome lilac-mauve flowers in early spring. Although only about 4 inches tall, plants are wonderfully ornamental and eye catching. Native as far north as Greenland, they also do well in southern climes. In my garden, plants flower as early as March 1 and persist for about six weeks. Provide some shade, fertilize a little in the spring, and sit back and enjoy. Plants may be divided at any time.

ODORATA (O-DO-RAH-TA)
Sweet Violet
Colors: Various
Zones: 6 to 8

Wonderfully fragrant flowers are produced over light green foliage in February and March. From flower markets in ancient Athens, Greece, to the large acreage planted in Europe until the 1950s to serve the perfume industry, plants have been produced for their soporific fragrance. When you plant a sweet violet, you plant centuries of history with it. The spurred flowers are only about ¾ inch wide and generally in some shade of violet. Plants spread by stolons and the leaves are slightly hairy. I plant them among the rocks around the garden pond, but unfortunately there

is too much shade for an abundance of flowers. I end up picking them as fast as they are produced anyway.

Cultivars

'Czar' has deep violet flowers, 'Queen Charlotte' produces dark blue blossoms, and 'Rosina' bears rose-pink flowers. Dozens of cultivars have been selected, and although they are not readily available, most specialty nurseries likely carry many of them.

PEDATA (PE-DAH-TA)
Bird's-foot Violet
Color: Lavender-violet
Zones: 4 to 8

The palmately divided leaves are quite distinctive and resemble a bird's foot, more or less. The feet are not nearly as handsome as the lavender-violet flowers that appear in the spring atop 4- to 6-inch-tall plants. Plants tolerate deep shade (they are woodland violets), but perform with more aplomb in areas of dappled shade. Good drainage is essential.

Cultivars

Var. *alba* bears flowers that contrast well with the foliage.

'Artist's Palette' bears lavender and white bicolored flowers up to 2 inches across. A most handsome selection from Don Jacobs of Eco Gardens, Decataur, Georgia.

Var. *concolor* has larger violet flowers with white markings at the base. A southern variety, it does very well in Zones 6 to 8.

ZEPHYRANTHES
(ZE-FI-RANTH-EEZ)
Zephyr Lily
Zones: 6 to 10

The zephyr lily consists of approximately 30 bulbous species, most of which are spring or fall flowering. Native from the Americas, mainly Mexico, Colombia, Guatemala, and the southeastern United States. Flower color is mainly white, although some species may be flushed with pink or rose and at least one species has yellow flowers (*Z. citrina*). None is particularly winter hardy and they shouldn't be left in the ground north of Zone 7. In northern areas, they may be lifted and stored just like gladioli and dahlias. The most impressive species is the Atamasco or swamp lily (*Z. atamasco*), native from Virginia to Florida and west to Mississippi. The white flowers, tinged with pink and about 3 inches wide, are produced in early to mid-spring. The bright shiny green leaves are strap shaped and up to 14 inches long. Place bulbs in partially shaded, damp areas—although I have seen some grown in regular garden beds in bright sun. They should not be allowed to dry out or flowers will not persist. Lift bulbs after the first frost and store in peat moss where they won't freeze. *Z. grandiflora*, the rose-pink zephyr lily or fairy lily, while perhaps not the most impressive, is probably the most delightful species. The large flowers are borne on 7-inch flower stems during the summer. Flowers appear like magic after summer rain and are sometimes known as rain lilies. They are hardy in Florida but make wonderful container plants on patios anywhere.

Nestled in the shaded garden or in full sun along the roadside, the flowers of the Atamasco lily, Zephyranthes atamasco, never fail to please.

SOME USER-FRIENDLY LISTS

Whenever I speak with people individually or in a group, inevitably the questions of sun/shade, wet/dry, heat/cold and other site-related queries arise. I don't particularly like a "shopper's list" of plants for various uses or sites because soils, rainfall, humidity and other factors all affect the success or failure of a plant in a given area. However, I have put together a few lists based on my observation of plants across the country; because of the size of this country, the lists that follow must be somewhat general. All lists include only the species covered in this book. Again, they are only guidelines, not meant to be gospel!

Plants for the Winter Garden

From lingering seed heads to foliage that relishes the winter cold, a number of plants possess a certain winter charm. More perennials may be enjoyed in the southern winter than in its northern counterpart, but you don't have to relinquish control completely to Old Man Winter in *any* part of the country.

Ajuga reptans	Bugleweed
Arum italicum 'Pictum', 'Marmoratum'	Arum
Asarum spp.	Wild ginger
Digitalis purpurea	Foxglove
Galeobdolon luteus	Yellow archangel
Heuchera americana	Alum root
Helleborus foetidus	Stinking hellebore
Helleborus orientalis	Lenten rose
Iberis sempervirens	Candytuft
Iris sibirica	Siberian iris
Iris tectorum	Japanese root iris
Liriope spicata	Gayfeather
Sedum 'Autumn Joy'	Autumn Joy Sedum
Stachys byzantina	Lamb's ears
Viola labradorica	Labrador violet

Plants with Persistent Flowering (6 weeks or longer)

Many perennials have flower interest for months at a time, and the following species catch the eye for many weeks. They don't throw only an occasional flower; rather, they just keep on partying. Removing spent flowers results in more persistent flowers with almost all species. Plants in the Northeast and Northwest tend to persist longer than those where high temperatures consistently occur.

Acanthus balcanicus	Bear's breeches
Acanthus mollis	Lady's-mantle
Achillea (most forms)	Yarrow
Anemonella thalictroides	Rue anemone
Aquilegia canadensis	Canadian columbine
Aster × *frikartii*	Frikart's aster
Aster tataricus	Tatarian aster
Brunnera macrophylla	Brunnera
Ceratostigma plumbaginoides	Leadwort
Coreopsis auriculata 'Nana'	Dwarf tickseed
Coreopsis grandiflora 'Sunray'	Common tickseed
Coreopsis 'Moonbeam'	Moonbeam coreopsis
Coreopsis verticillata	Threadleaf coreopsis
Dianthus gratianopolitanus	Cheddar pinks
Echinacea purpurea	Purple cone flower
Gaillardia × *grandiflora* 'Baby Cole', 'Goblin'	Blanket flower
Gaura lindheimeri	Gaura
Geranium sanguineum	Bloody cranesbill
Helleborus foetidus	Stinking hellebore
Helleborus orientalis	Lenten rose
Hemerocallis 'Stella de Oro' (many others)	Daylily
Kalimeris pinnatifida	Japanese aster
Lysimachia clethroides	Gooseneck loosestrife
Oenothera speciosa	Evening primrose
Oenothera missouriensis	Missouri primose
Perovskia atriplicifolia	Russian sage
Phlox paniculata 'Eva Cullum', 'Franz Shubert', 'Mount Fuji'	Summer phlox
Physostegia virginiana (pink and rose colors persist longer than white forms)	Obedient plant
Platycodon grandiflorus	Balloonflower
Rudbeckia fulgida 'Goldsturm'	Goldsturm rudbeckia
Rudbeckia nitida	Shining coneflower

(continued)

Plants with Persistent Flowering *(continued)*

Salvia × superba 'May Night'	Hybrid sage
Scabiosa caucasica 'Butterfly Blue'	Pincushion flower
Sedum 'Autumn Joy'	Autumn Joy sedum
Verbena bonariensis	Brazilian verbena
Verbena canadensis	Canadian verbena
Veronica 'Goodness Grows'	Hybrid veronica
Veronica longifolia	Long-leaf veronica
Veronica 'Sunny Border Blue'	Hybrid veronica
Viola labradorica	Labrador violet

Plants for Wet Areas

Some species prefer to have their roots consistently wet, and are particularly useful for boggy areas or the edges of natural ponds and streams. The following plants tolerate such conditions, but may be equally happy in a "normal" garden setting.

Amsonia tabernaemontana	Blue star flower
Arisaema sikokiana	Japanese jack-in-the-pulpit
Aruncus dioicus	Goatsbeard
Astilbe (all species)	Astilbe
Astrantia major	Masterwort
Brunnera macrophylla	Brunnera
Chelone obliqua	Turtle head
Cimicifuga racemosa	Snakeroot
Helianthus angustifolia	Swamp sunflower
Houttuynia cordata	Chameleon plant
Iris ensata	Japanese iris
Iris pseudacorus	Yellow flag iris
Ligularia (all forms)	Ligularia
Lobelia cardinalis	Cardinal flower
Lysimachia clethroides	Gooseneck loosestrife
Monarda didyma	Bee-balm
Persicaria bistorta	Bistort
Primula japonica	Japanese primrose
Rudbeckia nitida	Shining coneflower

Plants Tolerant of Heavy Shade

The following plants may be planted in an area with deciduous trees such as oak and maple. In general, such areas are too shady for grass and may be covered in leaf litter. The higher the canopy, the more chance plants will succeed. Rain showers will likely not penetrate the canopy, and unless sufficient rain falls, plants must be watered by hand.

Anemonella thalictroides	Rue-anemone
Asarum (all species)	Wild ginger
Arisaema (all species)	Jack-in-the-pulpit
Brunnera macrophylla	Brunnera
Epimedium (all species)	Barrenwort
Galeobdolon luteus	Yellow archangel
Heuchera americana	Alum root
Hosta (all species)	Hosta
Mertensia virginica	Virginia bluebell
Polygonatum odoratum 'Variegatum'	Fragrant Solomon's seal
Stylophorum diphyllum	Wood poppy
Tiarella cordifolia	Foam flower
Trillium (all species)	Trillium
Viola labradorica	Labrador violet

Plants for Fragrance

Gardens should include treats not only for the eyes, but also for the nose. Plants with fragrant flowers and foliage add an oft-forgotten dimension to the garden. (One gardener's fragrance may be another gardener's stench.)

Allium (leaves)	Ornamental onion
Artemisia (leaves)	Artemisia
Asarum (leaves and roots)	Wild ginger
Achillea (leaves)	Yarrow
Convallaria majalis (flowers)	Lily-of-the-valley
Dianthus (flowers)	Pinks
Galium odoratum (leaves)	Bedstraw
Geranium macrorrhizum (leaves)	Bigroot geranium

(continued)

Plants for Fragrance *(continued)*

Hosta plantaginea (flowers)	Fragrant hosta
Houttuynia cordata (leaves)	Chameleon plant
Paeonia (flowers)	Peony
Perovskia atriplicifolia (leaves)	Russian sage
Salvia (leaves)	Sage
Santolina (leaves)	Lavender cotton
Viola odorata (flowers)	Sweet violet

Plants for Groundcovers

One may argue that all plants that spread could be classified as groundcovers. However, almost all plants spread out a little (or die), therefore only those species that grow low to the ground and spread rapidly are included.

Ajuga reptans	Bugleweed
Epimedium spp.	Barrenwort
Galeobdolon luteus	Yellow archangel
Geranium macrorrhizum	Bigroot geranium
Houttuynia cordata	Chameleon plant
Lamium maculatum	Dead nettle
Liriope spicata	Liriope
Lysimachia nummularia	Creeping Jenny
Oenothera speciosa	Evening primrose
Pachysandra spp.	Spurge
Santolina	Lavender cotton
Verbena canadensis	Canadian verbena
Viola labradorica	Labrador violet

Plants That Give Headaches and Heartburn

Some species seem innocent enough when planted but as soon as you turn your back, they take over every square inch of the garden. In the right site these are fine plants; however, they don't belong in the display garden. One gardener's treasure may be another's weed.

Ajuga reptans	Bugleweed
Anemone vitifolia (tomentosa)	Grape leaf anemone
Aquilegia canadensis	Canadian columbine
Helianthus angustifolius	Swamp sunflower
Houttuynia cordata	Chameleon plant
Macleaya cordata	Plume poppy
Monarda didyma	Bee-balm
Oenothera speciosa	Showy evening primrose
Ornithogalum umbellatum	Star-of-Bethlehem
Physostegia virginiana ('Vivid' is better behaved than most)	Obedient plant
Polygonum cuspidatum	Mexican bamboo

Plants Grown Primarily for Foliage

Numerous plants are chosen first and foremost for their delightful foliage, although their flowers may be equally handsome. Cultivars with variegated foliage and bronze foliage are examples of these.

Artemisia spp.	Artemisia
Asarum shuttleworthii 'Callaway'	Callaway ginger
Cimicifuga ramosa 'Brunette', 'Atropurpurea'	Bronze snakeroot
Epimedium × *rubrum*	Red barrenwort
Heuchera americana	Alum root
Heuchera 'Palace Purple'	Palace purple heuchera
Hosta (all)	Hosta
Lamium maculatum 'White Nancy'	White Nancy nettle
Macleaya cordata	Plume poppy
Phlox paniculata 'Norah Leigh'	Norah Leigh phlox
Polygonatum odoratum 'Variegatum'	Variegated Solomon's seal
Salvia argentea	Silver sage
Santolina chamaecyparissus	Lavender cotton
Sisyrinchium striatum 'Aunt May'	Variegated sisyrinchium
Stachys byzantina	Lamb's ears

Plants for Extended Periods of Hot Weather

Many temperate-area perennials struggle in areas with long periods of warm weather, such as the deep southern states. However, some plants thrive in such heat. Many other species from tropical areas, not grown in other parts of the country, are the envy of gardeners everywhere,

Achillea millefolium	Common yarrow
Achillea filipendulina	Fern leaf yarrow
Chrysanthemum × superbum	Shasta daisy
Coreopsis grandiflora	Common tickseed
Echinacea purpurea	Purple cone flower
Gaillarda × grandiflora	Blanket flower
Hemerocallis spp.	Daylily
Physostegia virginiana	Obedient plant
Rudbeckia spp.	Yellow cone flower
Stokesia laevis	Stoke's aster
Verbena spp.	Verbena

Plants Tolerant of Dry Shade

Dry, shaded areas are some of the most difficult sites to fill. The most difficult places are those where the shade is the result of large shade trees whose roots suck out all the available water from beneath and around the trees. No plants enjoy such conditions, but a few will tolerate them. Provide additional irrigation whenever possible.

Alchemilla mollis	Lady's-mantle
Epimedium versicolor 'Sulphureum'	Barrenwort
Galeobdolon luteum	Yellow archangel
Lamium maculatum	Dead nettle
Polygonatum odoratum 'Variegatum'	Fragrant Solomon's seal
Viola labradorica	Labrador violet

Plants for Cutting

Plants used for cut flowers need not be shunted to the "cutting garden" but can and should be incorporated in the main garden. Without doubt, flowers from almost any plant can be cut and used indoors. The plants listed below are those with a vase life of at least 7 days in water. For best vase life, cut flowers in the morning and immediately plunge stems in water. The use of a flower preservative is highly recommended.

Achillea 'Coronation Gold'	Coronation gold yarrow
Achillea filipendulina	Fernleaf yarrow
Acidanthera bicolor	Abyssinian gladiolus
Alchemilla mollis	Lady's-mantle
Allium spp.	Ornamental onion
Anchusa azurea	Anchusa
Anemone coronaria	Poppy anemone
Aster spp.	Aster
Astilbe spp.	Astilbe
Baptisia australis	False blue indigo
Campanula persicifolia	Peachleaf bellflower
Campanula glomerata	Clustered bellflower
Convallaria majalis	Lily-of-the-valley
Delphinium spp.	Delphinium
Echinops ritro	Globe flower
Eryngium alpinum	Sea holly
Gypsophila paniculata	Baby's breath
Helleborus spp.	Hellebore
Iris ensata	Japanese iris
Iris foetidissima	Stinking iris
Liatris spicata	Gayfeather
Lysimachia clethroides	Gooseneck loosestrife
Phlox maculata	Spotted phlox
Phlox paniculata	Summer phlox
Physostegia virginiana	Obedient plant
Platycodon grandiflorus	Balloonflower
Scabiosa caucasica	Pincushion flower
× *Solidaster luteus*	Golden aster
Tricyrtis formosana	Toad lily
Veronica longifolia	Long-leaf veronica
Veronicastrum virginicum	Culver's root

THE USDA PLANT HARDINESS MAP OF THE UNITED STATES

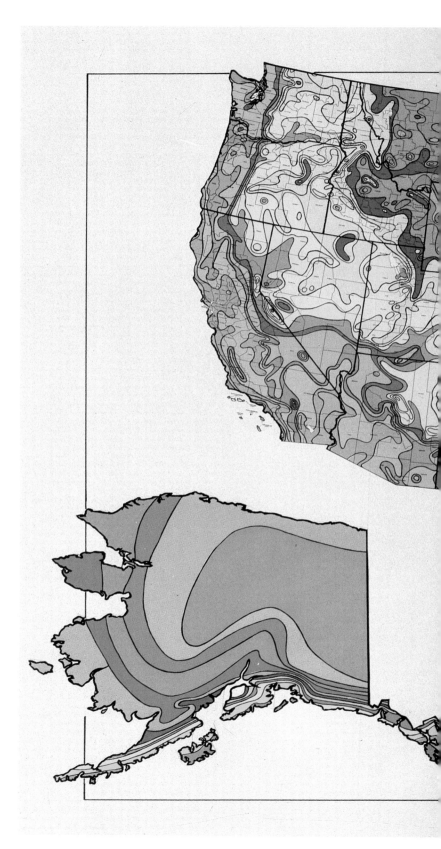

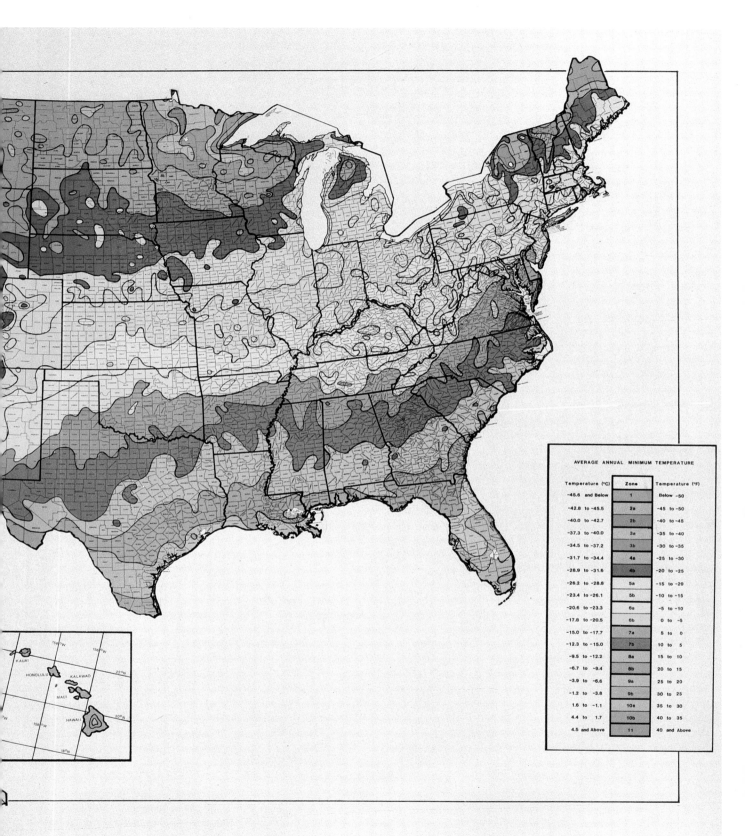

AVERAGE ANNUAL MINIMUM TEMPERATURE

Temperature (°C)	Zone	Temperature (°F)
-45.6 and Below	1	Below -50
-42.8 to -45.5	2a	-45 to -50
-40.0 to -42.7	2b	-40 to -45
-37.3 to -40.0	3a	-35 to -40
-34.5 to -37.2	3b	-30 to -35
-31.7 to -34.4	4a	-25 to -30
-28.9 to -31.6	4b	-20 to -25
-26.2 to -28.8	5a	-15 to -20
-23.4 to -26.1	5b	-10 to -15
-20.6 to -23.3	6a	-5 to -10
-17.8 to -20.5	6b	0 to -5
-15.0 to -17.7	7a	5 to 0
-12.3 to -15.0	7b	10 to 5
-9.5 to -12.2	8a	15 to 10
-6.7 to -9.4	8b	20 to 15
-3.9 to -6.6	9a	25 to 20
-1.2 to -3.8	9b	30 to 25
1.6 to -1.1	10a	35 to 30
4.4 to 1.7	10b	40 to 35
4.5 and Above	11	40 and Above

INDEX

Note: Italicized page numbers refer to captions.